AA POCKET PHRASE BOOK

SPANISH

D1434467

Contents

English edition prepared by First Edition Translations Ltd, Great Britain

Designed and produced by AA Publishing

Distributed in the United Kingdom by AA Publishing, Norfolk House, Priestley Road, Basingstoke, Hampshire RG24 9NY

First published in 1995 as Wat & Hoe Spaans, © Uitgeverij Kosmos bv – Utrecht/Antwerpen

Van Dale Lexicografie bv – Utrecht/Antwerpen

This edition © Automobile Association Developments Ltd 2000

A CIP catalogue record for this book is available from the British Library

ISBN: 0 7495 2143 0

Published by AA Publishing (a trading name of Automobile Association Developments Limited, whose registered office is Norfolk House, Priestley Road, Basingstoke, Hampshire RG24 9NY. Registered number 1878835).

Typeset by Anton Graphics Ltd, Andover, Hampshire.

Printed and bound by G. Canale & C., Turin, Italy.

Cover photograph: Casares, Costa del Sol, AA Photo Library (J.A. Tims)

Find out more about AA Publishing and the wide range of services the AA provides by visiting our web site at www.theaa.co.uk

Introduction

● **Welcome to the AA's new Essential Phrase Books series, covering the most popular European languages and containing everything you'd expect from a comprehensive language series. They're concise, accessible and easy to understand, and you'll find them indispensable on your trip abroad.**

Each guide is divided into 15 themed sections and starts with a pronunciation table which explains the phonetic pronunciation to all the words and phrases you'll need to know for your trip, while at the back of the book is an extensive word list and grammar guide which will help you construct basic sentences in your chosen language.

Throughout the book you'll come across coloured boxes with a 🌐 beside them. These are designed to help you if you can't understand what your listener is saying to you. Hand the book over to them and encourage them to point to the appropriate answer to the question you are asking.

Other coloured boxes in the book – this time without the symbol – give alphabetical listings of themed words with their English translations beside them.

For extra clarity, we have put all English words and phrases in black, foreign language terms in red and their phonetic pronunciation in italic.

This phrase book covers all subjects you are likely to come across during the course of your visit, from reserving a room for the night to ordering food and drink at a restaurant and what to do if your car breaks down or you lose your traveller's cheques and money. With over 2,000 commonly used words and essential phrases at your fingertips you can rest assured that you will be able to get by in all situations, so let the Essential Phrase Book become your passport to a secure and enjoyable trip!

Pronunciation table

The pronunciation provided should be read as if it were English, bearing in mind the following main points:

Vowels

Vowels in Spanish are very open

a	is like a in amber,	*ah*	as in **casa**	*kahsah*
e	is like e in egg,	*eh*	as in **esta**	*ehstah*
i	is like ee in seen,	*ee*	as in **isla**	*eeslah*
o	is like o in John,	*oh*	as in **hotel**	*ohtehl*
u	is like oo in room,	*oo*	as in **uno**	*oonoh*
y	is like ee in seen,	*ee*	as in **y**	*ee*
	the diphthong **ay** is pronounced as in aisle or eye			
			as in **hay**	*eye*

Consonants

Consonants are as in English, pronounced less clearly, except

b/v	are pronounced roughly the same		
		as in **vamos**	*bahmohs*
c	before e and i is soft and is like the **th** in tha**tch**		
		as in **la acera**	*lah ahthehrah*
	before a,o and u is hard		
		as in **cosa**	*kohsah*
cu	before another vowel is pronounced like **cw**		
		as in **la cuenta**	*lah kwehntah*
g	before e and i is soft and is like the Scottish **ch** in lo**ch**,		
		as in **la gente**	*lah <u>h</u>ehnteh*
	before a, o and u is hard		
		as in **gato**	*ghahtoh*
gu	before e and i is pronounced as hard **g**		
		as in **la guía**	*geeah*
	before a, o and u is pronounced like **gw**		
		as in **guapo**	*gwahpoh*
gü	before e and i is pronounced like **gw**		
		as in **lingüística**	*leengwees-teekah*
h	is silent		
j	is like the soft g	as in **jarra**	*<u>h</u>ahrrah*
ll	is like lli in billion	as in **llave**	*lyahbeh*
ñ	is like ni in onion	as in **año**	*ahnyoh*
r	is rolled as in the Scottish **r**, **rr** is a longer roll		
z	is like **th** in thought	as in **taza**	*tahthah*

The stress normally falls on the last syllable of the word (**hotel**), except that words ending in a vowel (not including **y**) or in n or s (**casa**, **casas**) are stressed on the next to the last syllable. All exceptions are indicated by a written acute accent (**Córdoba**, *kohrdohbah*).

Note: In the south, the soft **c** and the **z** are pronounced *s*. This is also true in Latin America.

Useful lists

Useful lists

1.1 **T**oday or tomorrow?

What day is it today? _____ ¿Qué día es hoy?
keh deeah ehs oy?

Today's Monday _____ Hoy es lunes
oy ehs loonehs

– Tuesday _____ Hoy es martes
oy ehs mahrtehs

– Wednesday _____ Hoy es miércoles
oy ehs myehrkohlehs

– Thursday _____ Hoy es jueves
oy ehs <u>h</u>ooehbehs

– Friday _____ Hoy es viernes
oy ehs byehrnehs

– Saturday _____ Hoy es sábado
oy ehs sahbahdoh

– Sunday _____ Hoy es domingo
oy ehs dohmeengoh

in January _____ en enero
ehn ehnehroh

since February _____ desde febrero
dehsdeh fehbrehroh

in spring _____ en primavera
ehn preemahbehrah

in summer _____ en verano
ehn behrahnoh

in autumn _____ en otoño
ehn ohtohnyoh

in winter _____ en invierno
ehn eenbyehrno

1997 _____ mil novecientos noventa y siete
meel nohbehthyentohs nohbehntah ee syehteh

the twentieth century _____ el siglo XX (veinte)
ehl seegloh beheenteh

What's the date today? _____ ¿Qué día es hoy?
keh deeah ehs oy?

Today's the 24th _____ Hoy es 24 (veinticuatro)
oy ehs beheenteekwahtroh

Monday 3 November 1998 _____ lunes 3 (tres) de noviembre de 1998 (mil
novecientos noventa y ocho)
*loonehs trehs deh nohbyehmbreh deh meel
nohbehthyehntohs nohbehntah ee ohchoh*

in the morning _____ por la mañana
pohr lah mahnyahnah

in the afternoon _____ por la tarde
pohr lah tahrdeh

in the evening _____ por la noche
pohr lah nohcheh

at night _____ por la noche
pohr lah nohcheh

this morning _____ esta mañana
ehstah mahnyahnah

this afternoon	esta tarde *ehstah tahrdeh*
this evening	esta noche *ehstah nohcheh*
tonight	esta noche *ehstah nohcheh*
last night	anoche *ahnohcheh*
this week	esta semana *ehstah sehmahnah*
next month	el mes próximo *ehl mehs prohxeemoh*
last year	el año pasado *ehl ahnyo pahsahdoh*
next...	el/la... próximo/a *ehl/lah... prohxeemoh/ah*
in...days/weeks/ months/years	dentro de...días/semanas/meses/años *dehntroh deh...* *deeahs/sehmahnahs/mehsehs/ahnyohs*
...weeks ago	hace...semanas *ahthe...sehmahnahs*
day off	día libre *deeah leebreh*

 .2 Bank Holidays

● **The most important** Bank Holidays in Spain are the following:

January 1	New Year's Day (Año Nuevo)
January 6	Epiphany (Epifanía)
March 19	St. Joseph's Day (San José)
March/April	Good Friday (Viernes Santo)
March/April	Easter Monday(Catalonia) (Lunes Santo)
May 1	Labour Day (Día del Trabajo)
May/June	Corpus Christi (Corpus Christi)
July 25	St. James's Day (Santiago)
August 15	Assumption Day (Asunción)
October 12	Columbus Day (Día de las Américas)
November 1	All Saints' Day (Todos los Santos)
December 6	Constitution Day (Día de la Constitución)
December 8	Immaculate Conception (Inmaculada Concepción)
December 25	Christmas (Navidad)

There are also various regional holidays like San Fermín in Pamplona (July 6-13) and the Fallas in Valencia (March 19).

.3 What time is it?

What time is it?	¿Qué hora es? *keh ohrah ehs?*
It's nine o'clock	Son las nueve *sohn lahs nwehbeh*
– five past ten	Son las diez y cinco *sohn lahs dyeth ee theenkoh*
– a quarter past eleven	Son las once y cuarto *sohn lahs ohntheh ee kwahrtoh*
– twenty past twelve	Son las doce y veinte *sohn lahs dohthe ee beheenteh*

– half past one	Es la una y media *ehs lah oonah ee mehdyah*
– twenty–five to three	Son las tres menos veinticinco *sohn lahs trehs mehnohs beheenteetheenkoh*
– a quarter to four	Son las cuatro menos cuarto *sohn lahs kwahtroh mehnohs kwahrtoh*
– ten to five	Son las cinco menos diez *sohn lahs theenkoh mehnohs dyehth*
– twelve noon	Son las doce del mediodía *sohn lahs dohtheh dehl mehdyohdeeah*
– midnight	Son las doce de la noche *sohn lahs dohtheh deh lah nohcheh*
half an hour	media hora *mehdyah ohrah*
What time?	¿A qué hora? *ah keh ohrah?*
What time can I come round?	¿A qué hora puedo pasar? *ah keh ohrah pwehdoh pahsahr?*
At...	A las... *ah lahs...*
After...	Después de las... *dehspwehs deh lahs...*
Before...	Antes de las... *ahntehs deh lahs...*
Between...and...	Entre las...y las... *ehntreh lahs...ee lahs...*
From...to...	De las...a las... *deh lahs...ah lahs...*
In...minutes	Dentro de...minutos *dehntroh deh...meenootohs*
– an hour	Dentro de una hora *dehntroh deh oonah ohrah*
– ...hours	Dentro de...horas *dehntroh deh...ohrahs*
– a quarter of an hour	Dentro de un cuarto de hora *dehntroh deh oon kwahrtoh deh ohrah*
– three quarters of an hour	Dentro de tres cuartos de hora *dehntroh deh trehs kwahrtohs deh ohrah*
early/late	muy temprano/tarde *mwee tehmprahnoh/tahrdeh*
on time	a tiempo *ah tyehmpoh*
summer opening hours	horario de verano *ohrahryoh deh behrahnoh*
winter opening hours	horario de invierno *ohrahryoh deh eenbyehrnoh*

1 .4 One, two, three...

0	cero	*thehroh*
1	uno	*oonoh*
2	dos	*dohs*
3	tres	*trehs*
4	cuatro	*kwahtroh*

5	cinco	*theenkoh*
6	seis	*sehees*
7	siete	*syehteh*
8	ocho	*ohchoh*
9	nueve	*nwehbeh*
10	diez	*dyeth*
11	once	*ohntheh*
12	doce	*dohtheh*
13	trece	*trehtheh*
14	catorce	*kahtohrtheh*
15	quince	*keentheh*
16	dieciséis	*dyetheesehees*
17	diecisiete	*dyetheesyehteh*
18	dieciocho	*dyetheeohchoh*
19	diecinueve	*dyetheenwehbe*
20	veinte	*beheenteh*
21	veintiuno	*beheenteeoonoh*
22	veintidós	*beheenteheedohs*
30	treinta	*treheentah*
31	treinta y uno	*treheentah ee oonoh*
32	treinta y dos	*treheentah ee dohs*
40	cuarenta	*kwahrehntah*
50	cincuenta	*theenkwehntah*
60	sesenta	*sehsehntah*
70	setenta	*sehtehntah*
80	ochenta	*ohchehntah*
90	noventa	*nohvehntah*
100	cien	*thyehn*
101	ciento uno	*thyehntoh oonoh*
110	ciento diez	*thyehntoh dyeth*
120	ciento veinte	*thyehntoh beheenteh*
200	doscientos	*dohsthyehntohs*
300	trescientos	*trehsthyehntohs*
400	cuatrocientos	*kwahtrohthyehntohs*
500	quinientos	*keenyehntohs*
600	seiscientos	*seheesthyehntohs*
700	setecientos	*sehtehthyehntohs*
800	ochocientos	*ohchohthyehntohs*
900	novecientos	*nohbehthyentohs*
1000	mil	*meel*
1100	mil cien	*meel thyehn*
2000	dos mil	*dohs meel*
10,000	diez mil	*dyeth meel*
100,000	cien mil	*thyehn meel*
1,000,000	un millón	*oon meelyohn*
1st	primero	*preemehroh*
2nd	segundo	*sehgoondoh*
3rd	tercero	*tehrthehroh*
4th	cuarto	*kwahrtoh*
5th	quinto	*keentoh*
6th	sexto	*sehxtoh*
7th	séptimo	*sehpteemoh*
8th	octavo	*ohktahboh*

9th	noveno	*nohvehnoh*
10th	décimo	*dehtheemoh*
11th	undécimo	*oondehtheemoh*
12th	duodécimo	*doo-ohdehtheemo*
13th	decimotercero	*dehtheemohtehrthehroh*
14th	decimocuarto	*dehtheemohkwahrtoh*
15th	decimoquinto	*dehtheemohkeentoh*
16th	decimosexto	*dehtheemohsehxtoh*
17th	decimoséptimo	*dehtheemosehpteemoh*
18th	decimoctavo	*dehtheemohktahboh*
19th	decimonoveno	*dehtheemonobenoh*
20th	vigésimo	*beeheseemoh*
21st	vigesimoprimero	*beeheseemohpreemeroh*
22nd	vigesimosegundo	*beeheseemohsegoondoh*
30th	trigésimo	*treeheseemoh*
100th	centésimo	*thentehseemoh*
1,000th	milésimo	*meelehseemoh*

once	una vez	*oonah behth*
twice	dos veces	*dos behthes*
double	el doble	*ehl dohbleh*
triple	el triple	*ehl treepleh*
half	la mitad	*lah meetath*
a quarter	un cuarto	*oon kwartoh*
a third	un tercio	*oon terthyoh*
a couple, a few, some	unos, algunos	*oonohs, algoonohs*

2 + 4 = 6	dos más cuatro, seis	*dohs mahs kwahtroh, sehees*
4 – 2 = 2	cuatro menos dos, dos	*kwahtroh mehnohs dohs, dohs*
2 x 4 = 8	dos por cuatro, ocho	*dohs pohr kwahtroh, ohchoh*
4 ÷ 2 = 2	cuatro dividido dos, dos	*kwahtroh deebeedeedoh dohs, dohs*

odd/even	par/impar	*pahr/eempahr*
total	(en) total	*(ehn) tohtahl*
6 x 9	seis por nueve	*sehees pohr nwehbeh*

1 .5 The weather

Is the weather going to be good/bad?	¿Hará buen/mal tiempo? *ahrah bwehn/mahl tyehmpoh?*
Is it going to get colder/hotter?	¿Hará más frío/calor? *ahrah mahs freeoh/kahlohr?*

What temperature is it going to be?	¿Cuántos grados hará?
	kwahntohs grahdohs ahrah?
Is it going to rain?	¿Va a llover?
	bah ah lyohbehr?
Is there going to be a storm?	¿Tendremos tormenta?
	tehndrehmohs tohrmehntah?
Is it going to snow?	¿Va a nevar?
	bah ah nehbahr?
Is it going to freeze?	¿Va a helar?
	bah ah ehlahr?
Is the thaw setting in?	¿Comenzará el deshielo?
	kohmehnzahrah ehl dehsyeloh
Is it going to be foggy?	¿Habrá niebla?
	ahbrah nyehblah?
Is there going to be a thunderstorm?	¿Habrá tormenta eléctrica?
	ahbrah tohrmehntah ehlehktreekah?
The weather's changing	Va a cambiar el tiempo
	bah ah kahmbyahr ehl tyehmpoh
It's cooling down	Va a refrescar
	bah ah rehfrehskahr
What's the weather going to be like today/tomorrow?	¿Qué tiempo hará hoy/mañana?
	keh tyehmpoh ahrah oy/mahnyahnah?

algo nublado/nublado light/heavy clouds	granizo hail	ola de calor heat wave
bochornoso stormy	...grados(bajo/sobre cero) ...degrees(above/ below zero)	pesado muggy
bueno fine	helada (black) ice	sofocante scorching hot
caluroso hot	húmedo damp	soleado sunny
chubasco shower	huracán hurricane	suave mild
cielo cubierto overcast	llovizna drizzle	tormenta eléctrica thunderstorm
desapacible bleak	lluvia rain	vendaval gale
despejado clear	lluvioso wet	ventoso windy
escarcha frost	niebla fog	viento wind
fresco chilly	nieve snow	viento leve /moderado/ fuerte light/moderate/ strong wind
frìo cold	nublado cloudy	tempestad squall

Useful lists

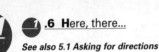

1.6 Here, there...

See also 5.1 Asking for directions

here/there _____	aquí/allá
	ahkee/ahlyah
somewhere/nowhere _____	en alguna/ninguna parte
	ehn algoonah/neengoonah pahrteh
everywhere _____	en todas partes
	ehn tohdahs pahrtehs
far away/nearby _____	lejos/cerca
	lehhos/thehrkah
right/left _____	a la derecha/izquierda
	ah lah dehrehchah/eethkyehrdah
to the right/left of _____	a la derecha/izquierda de
	ah lah dehrehchah/eethkyehrdah deh
straight ahead _____	todo recto
	tohdoh rehktoh
via _____	pasando por
	pahsahndoh pohr
in _____	en
	ehn
on_____	sobre
	sohbreh
under _____	debajo de
	dehbahhoh deh
against _____	contra
	kohntrah
opposite_____	frente a
	frehnteh ah
next to _____	al lado de
	ahl lahdoh deh
near_____	junto a
	hoontoh ah
in front of_____	delante de
	dehlahnteh deh
in the centre _____	en el medio
	ehn ehl mehdyoh
forward_____	hacia adelante
	ahthyah ahdehlanteh
down_____	(hacia) abajo
	(ahthyah) ahbahhoh
up_____	(hacia) arriba
	(ahthya) ahrreebah
inside _____	(hacia) adentro
	(ahthya) ahdehntroh
outside _____	(hacia) afuera
	(ahthya) ahfwehrah
behind _____	(hacia) atrás
	(ahthya) ahtrahs
at the front _____	delante
	dehlahnteh
at the back_____	detrás
	dehtrahs
in the north _____	en el norte
	ehn ehl nohrteh

to the south_____	hacia el sur	
	ahthya ehl soor	
from the west_____	del oeste	
	dehl ohehsteh	
from the east _____	del este	
	dehl ehsteh	
...of _____	al...de	
	ahl...deh	

.7 What does that sign say?

See 5.4 Traffic signs

abierto/cerrado	horario (de apertura)	prohibido pisar el
open/closed	**opening hours**	césped
agua no potable	información	**keep off the grass**
no drinking water	**information**	razón aquí
alta tensión	liquidación (por	**inquiries**
high voltage	cese)	rebajas
ascensor	**closing-down sale**	**clearance**
lift	no funciona	recepción
caballeros	**out of order**	**reception**
gents/gentlemen	no tocar	recién pintado
caja	**please do not touch**	**wet paint**
pay here	peligro	reservado
completo	**danger**	**reserved**
full	peligro de incendio	saldos
coto privado	**fire hazard**	**sale**
private (property)	...piso	salida
cuidado con el perro	**...floor**	**exit**
beware of the dog	primeros auxilios	salida de
cuidado, escalón	**first aid**	emergencia/salida
mind the step	prohibido el paso	de socorro
entrada	**no entry**	**emergency exit**
entrance	prohibido fotografiar	se alquila
entrada libre	**no photographs**	**for hire**
free admission	prohibido fumar	se ruega no molestar
escalera	**no smoking**	**do not disturb**
stairs	prohibido hacer	se vende
escalera de	fuego	**for sale**
incendios	**no open fires**	señoras
fire escape	prohibido para	**ladies**
escalera mecánica	animales	servicios
escalator	**no pets allowed**	**toilets**
freno de emergencia		empujar/tirar
emergency brake		**push/pull**

.8 Telephone alphabet

a	_____*ah*	de Antonio	*deh ahntohnyoh*
b	_____*beh*	de Barcelona	*deh bahr-thehlohnah*
c	_____*theh*	de Carmen	*deh kahrmehn*
ch	_____*cheh*	de chocolate	*deh chohkohlahteh*
d	_____*deh*	de Dolores	*deh dohlohrehs*

e	eh	de Enrique	deh ehnreekeh
f	hefeh	de Francia	deh frahnthyah
g	heh	de Gerona	de hehrohnah
h	ahcheh	de historia	de eestohryah
i	ee	de Inés	deh eenehs
j	hohtah	de José	deh hohseh
k	kah	de Kilo	deh keeloh
l	ehleh	de Lorenzo	deh lohrehnthoh
ll	ehlyeh	de Llobregat	deh lyohbrehgaht
m	ehmeh	de Madrid	deh Mahdreedh
n	ehneh	de Navarra	deh nahbahrrah
ñ	ehnyeh	de ñoño	deh nyohnyoh
o	oh	de Oviedo	deh ohbyedoh
p	peh	de París	deh pahrees
q	koo	de querido	deh kehreedoh
r	ehrreh	de Ramón	deh rahmohn
s	ehseh	de sábado	deh sahbahdoh
t	teh	de Tarragona	deh tahrrahgohnah
u	oo	de Ulises	deh ooleesehs
v	oobeh	de Valencia	deh bahlehnthyah
w	oobehdohbleh	de Washington	deh wahsheengtohn
x	ehkees	de Xiquena	deh heekehnah
y	eegryehgah	griega	
z	thehtah	de Zaragoza	deh thahrrahgohthah

1 .9 Personal details

surname	apellidos	ahpehlyeedohs
christian name(s)	nombre	nohmbreh
initials	iniciales	eeneethyahlehs
address (street/number)	dirección (calle/número)	deerehkthyohn (kahlyeh/noomehroh)
post code/town	código postal/población	cohdeegoh pohstahl/pohblahthyon)
sex (male/female)	sexo (v = varón, m = mujer)	sehksoh (v = bahrohn, m = moohehr)
nationality	nacionalidad	nahthyohnahleedahdh
date of birth	fecha de nacimiento	fehchah deh nahtheemyehntoh
place of birth	lugar de nacimiento	loogahr deh natheemyehntoh
occupation	profesión	profehsyohn
married/single/divorced	casado, casada/soltero, soltera/ divorciado, divorciada	kahsahdoh, kahsahdah/sohltehroh, sohltehrah/deebohrthyahdoh, deebohrthyahdah
widowed	viuda/viudo	byoodah/byoodoh
(number of) children	(número de) hijos	(noomehroh deh) eehohs

passport/identity card/driving licence/ number, place and date of issue _____ pasaporte/carnet de identidad/permiso de conducir/número, lugar y fecha de expedición

kahrneh deh eedehnteedahdh (pahsahpohrteh/pehrmeesoh deh kohndootheer) noomehroh, loogahr ee fehchah deh ehkspehdeethyohn

2

Courtesies

Courtesies

● **Female friends and relatives** kiss on both cheeks in Spain.
In shops, etc., you will hear ¡Buenos días! or just ¡Buenas!, and expect
to be addressed in Basque or Catalan in these provinces. For example
you will hear ¡Agur! instead of ¡Adiós! in the Basque Country.

 .1 Greetings

Hello, Mr Smith _____	Hola, buenos días
	ohlah, bwehnohs deeahs
Hello, Peter _____	Hola, Pedro
	ohlah, pehdroh
Hi, Helen _____	Qué hay, Elena
	keh ay, ehlehnah
Good morning, madam____	Buenos días, señora (before 2pm)
	bwehnohs deeahs, sehnyohrah
Good afternoon, sir _____	Buenas tardes, señor (after 2pm)
	bwehnahs tahrdehs, sehnyohr
Good evening_____	Buenas tardes (before 9pm), buenas
	noches (after 9pm)
	bwehnahs tahrdehs, bwehnahs nohchehs
How are you? _____	¿Qué tal?
	keh tahl?
Fine, thank you, and you?__	Muy bien, ¿y usted?
	mwee byehn, ee oostehdh?
Very well _____	Estupendo
	ehstoopehndoh
Not very well _____	Regular
	rehgoolahr
Not too bad_____	Tirando
	teerando
I'd better be going_____	Bueno, me voy
	bwehnoh, meh boy
I have to be going. _____	Tengo que irme. Me están esperando
Someone's waiting	*tehngoh keh eermeh, meh ehstahn*
for me	*ehspehrahndoh*
Bye!_____	¡Adiós!
	ahdyohs!
Goodbye _____	Hasta luego
	ahstah lwehgoh
See you soon _____	Hasta pronto
	ahstah prohntoh
See you later _____	Hasta luego
	ahstah lwehgoh
See you in a little while ____	Hasta ahora
	ahstah ahohrah
Sleep well _____	Que descanse
	keh dehskahnseh
Good night _____	Buenas noches
	bwehnahs nohchehs
All the best _____	Que le vaya bien
	keh leh bahyah byehn
Have fun_____	Que se divierta, que lo pase bien
	keh seh deebyehrtah, keh loh pahseh byehn

Good luck	Mucha suerte
moochah swehrteh
Have a nice holiday	Felices vacaciones
fehleethehs bahkahthyohnehs
Have a good trip	Buen viaje
bwehn byahheh
Thank you, you too	Gracias, igualmente
grahthyahs, eegwahlmehnteh
Say hello to...for me	Recuerdos a...
rehkwehrdohs ah...

.2 How to ask a question

Who?	¿Quién?
kyehn?
Who's that?	¿Quién es?
kyehn ehs?
What?	¿Qué?
keh?
What's there to see here?	¿Qué se puede visitar aquí?
keh seh pwehdeh beeseetahr ahkee?
What kind of hotel is that?	¿Qué clase de hotel es?
keh klahseh deh ohtehl ehs?
Where?	¿Dónde?
dohndeh?
Where's the toilet?	¿Dónde están los servicios?
dohndeh ehstahn lohs sehrbeethyohs?
Where are you going?	¿A dónde va?
ahdohndeh bah?
Where are you from?	¿De dónde es usted?
deh dohndeh ehs oostehdh?
How?	¿Cómo?
kohmoh?
How far is that?	¿A qué distancia queda?
ah keh deestahnthyah kehdah?
How long does it take?	¿Cuánto dura?
kwahntoh doorah?
How long is the trip?	¿Cuánto dura el viaje?
kwahntoh doorah ehl byahheh?
How much?	¿Cuánto?
kwahntoh?
How much is this?	¿Cuánto vale?
kwahntoh bahleh?
What time is it?	¿Qué hora es?
keh ohrah ehs?
Which?	¿Cuál? ¿Cuáles?
kwahl? kwahlehs?
Which glass is mine?	¿Cuál es mi copa?
kwahl ehs mee kohpah?
When?	¿Cuándo?
kwahndoh?
When are you leaving?	¿Cuándo sale?
kwahndoh sahleh?
Why?	¿Por qué?
pohr keh?
Could you...me?	¿Podría...?
pohdreeah...?

Could you help me, _____ please?	¿Podría ayudarme? *pohdreeah ahyoodahrmeh?*
Could you point that_____ out to me?	¿Me lo podría indicar? *meh loh pohdreeah eendeekahr?*
Could you come _____ with me, please?	¿Le importaría acompañarme? *leh eempohrtahreeah ahkohmpahnyahrmeh?*
Could you..._____	¿Quiere...?/¿Podría...? *kyehreh...?/pohdreeah...?*
Could you reserve some ___ tickets for me, please?	¿Me podría reservar entradas? *meh pohdreeah rehsehrbahr ehntrahdahs?*
Do you know...? _____	¿Sabe...? *sahbeh...?*
Do you know another_____ hotel, please?	¿Sabría indicarme otro hotel? *sahbreeah eendeekahrmeh ohtroh ohtehl?*
Do you know whether...?___	¿Tiene...? *tyehneh...?*
Do you have a...?_____	¿Me podría dar un(a)...? *meh pohdreeah dahr oon(ah)...?*
Do you have a _____ vegetarian dish, please?	¿Tendría un plato sin carne? *tehndreeah oon plahtoh seen kahrneh?*
I'd like... _____	Quisiera... *keesyehrah...*
I'd like a kilo of apples, ___ please.	Quisiera un kilo de manzanas *keesyehrah oon keeloh deh mahnthahnahs*
Can I...?_____	¿Puedo...?/¿Se puede...? *pwehdoh...?/seh pwehdeh?*
Can I take this?_____	¿Podría llevármelo? *pohdreeah lyehbahrmehloh?*
Can I smoke here?_____	¿Se puede fumar aquí? *seh pwehdeh foomahr ahkee?*
Could I ask you _____ something?	¿Puedo hacerle una pregunta? *pwehdoh ahthehrleh oonah prehgoontah?*

2 .3 **H**ow to reply

Yes, of course_____	Sí, claro *see, klahroh*
No, I'm sorry_____	No, lo siento *noh, loh syehntoh*
Yes, what can I do _____ for you?	Sí. ¿En qué puedo servirle? *see, ehn keh pwehdoh sehrbeerleh?*
Just a moment, please ____	Un momento, por favor *oon mohmehntoh, pohr fahbohr*
No, I don't have _____ time now	No, ahora no tengo tiempo *noh, aohrah noh tehngoh tyehmpoh*
No, that's impossible _____	No, eso es imposible *noh, ehsoh ehs eempohseebleh*
I think so _____	Creo que sí *krehoh keh see*
I agree_____	Yo también lo creo *yoh tahmbyehn loh krehoh*
I hope so too_____	Yo también lo espero *yoh tahmbyehn loh ehspehroh*
No, not at all_____	No, de ninguna manera *noh, deh neengoonah mahnehrah*
No, no-one _____	No, nadie *noh, nahdyeh*

No, nothing	No, nada
	noh, nahdah
That's (not) right	(No) es cierto
	(noh) ehs thyehrtoh
I (don't) agree	(No) estoy de acuerdo con usted
	(noh) ehstoy deh ahkwehrdoh kohn oostehdh
All right	Está bien
	ehstah byehn
Okay	Vale
	bahleh
Perhaps	Quizá
	keethah
I don't know	No lo sé
	noh loh seh

2 .4 Thank you

Thank you	Gracias
	grahthyahs
You're welcome	De nada
	deh nahdah
Thank you very much	Muchísimas gracias
	moocheeseemahs grahthyahs
Very kind of you	Muy amable (de su parte)
	mwee ahmahbleh (deh soo pahrteh)
I enjoyed it very much	Ha sido un verdadero placer
	ah seedoh oon behrdahdehroh plahthehr
Thank you for your trouble	Gracias por la molestia
	grahthyahs pohr lah mohlehstyah
You shouldn't have	No se hubiera molestado
	noh seh oobyehrah mohlehstahdoh
That's all right	No se preocupe
	noh seh prehohkoopeh

2 .5 Sorry

Excuse me	Perdone
	pehrdohneh
Sorry!	¡Perdone!
	pehrdohneh!
I'm sorry, I didn't know...	Perdone, no sabía que...
	pehrdohneh, noh sahbeeah keh...
I do apologise	Perdone
	pehrdohneh
I'm sorry	Lo siento
	loh syehntoh
I didn't do it on purpose, it was an accident	No ha sido a propósito; ha sido sin querer
	noh ah seedoh ah prohpohseetoh; ah seedoh seen kehrehr
That's all right	No importa
	noh eempohrtah
Never mind	Déjelo
	dehhehloh
It could've happened to anyone	Le puede pasar a cualquiera
	leh pwehdeh pahsahr ah kwahlkyehrah

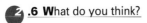

.6 What do you think?

Which do you prefer?	¿Qué prefiere?
	keh prehfyehreh?
What do you think?	¿Qué te parece?
	keh teh pahrehtheh?
Don't you like dancing?	¿No te gusta bailar?
	noh teh goostah bahylahr?
I don't mind	Me da igual
	meh dah eegwahl
Well done!	¡Muy bien!
	mwee byehn!
Not bad!	¡No está mal!
	noh ehstah mahl!
Great!	¡Excelente!
	ehxthehlehnteh!
Wonderful!	¡Qué delicia!
	keh dehleethyah!
It's really nice here!	¡Qué bien se está aquí!
	keh byehn seh ehstah ahkee!
How nice!	¡Qué mono/bonito!
	keh mohnoh/bohneetoh!
How nice for you!	¡Cuánto me alegro por usted!
	kwahntoh meh ahlehgroh pohr oostehdh!
I'm (not) very happy with...	(No) estoy muy contento con...
	(noh) ehstoy mwee kohntehntoh kohn...
I'm glad...	Me alegro de que...
	meh ahlehgroh deh keh...
I'm having a great time	Me lo estoy pasando muy bien
	meh loh ehstoy pahsahndoh mwee byehn
I'm looking forward to it	Me hace ilusión
	meh ahtheh eeloosyohn
I hope it'll work out	Espero que salga bien
	ehspehroh keh sahlgah byehn
That's ridiculous!	¡Qué ridículo!
	keh reedeekooloh!
That's terrible!	¡Qué horrible!
	keh ohrreebleh!
What a pity!	¡Qué lástima!
	keh lahsteemah!
That's filthy!	¡Qué asco!
	keh ahskoh!
What a load of rubbish!	¡Qué tontería!
	keh tohntehreeah!
I don't like...	No me gusta...
	noh meh goostah...
I'm bored to death	Me aburro como una ostra
	meh ahboorroh kohmoh oonah ohstrah
I've had enough	Estoy harto(a)
	ehstoy ahrtoh(ah)
This is no good	No puede ser
	noh pwehdeh sehr
I was expecting something completely different	Yo me había esperado otra cosa
	yoh meh ahbeeah ehspehrahdoh ohtrah kohsah

2

Courtesies

3

Conversation

Conversation

3.1 I beg your pardon?

I don't speak any/ _____ I speak a little...	No hablo/hablo un poco de... *noh ahbloh/ahbloh oon pohkoh deh...*
I'm English _____	Soy inglés/inglesa *soy eenglehs/eenglehsah*
I'm Scottish _____	Soy escocés/escocesa *soy ehskohthehs/ehskothehsah*
I'm Irish _____	Soy irlandés/irlandesa *soy eerlahndehs/eerlahndehsah*
I'm Welsh _____	soy galés/galesa *soy gahlehs/gahlehsah*
Do you speak _____ English/French/German?	¿Habla inglés/francés/alemán? *ahblah eenglehs/frahnthehs/ahlehmahn?*
Is there anyone who _____ speaks...?	¿Hay alguien que hable...? *ay ahlgyehn ahkee keh ahbleh...?*
I beg your pardon? _____	¿Cómo dice? *kohmoh deeteh?*
I (don't) understand _____	(No) comprendo *(noh) kohmprehndoh*
Do you understand me? ___	¿Me entiende? *meh ehntyehndeh?*
Could you repeat that, _____ please?	¿Le importa repetirlo? *leh eempohrtah rehpehteerloh?*
Could you speak more _____ slowly, please?	¿Podría hablar más despacio? *pohdreeah ahblahr mahs dehspahthyo?*
What does that (word) _____ mean?	¿Qué significa esto/esta palabra? *keh seegneefeekah ehstoh/ehstah pahlahbrah?*
Is that similar to/the _____ same as...?	¿Es (más o menos) lo mismo que...? *ehs mahs oh mehnohs loh meesmoh keh...?*
Could you write that _____ down for me, please?	¿Podría escribírmelo? *pohdreeah eskreebeermehloh?*
Could you spell that _____ for me, please? *(See 1.8 Telephone alphabet)*	¿Podría deletreármelo? *pohdreeah dehlehtrehahrmehloh?*
Could you point that _____ out in this phrase book, please?	¿Me lo podría señalar en esta guía? *meh loh pohdreeah sehnyahlahr ehn ehstah gheeah?*
One moment, please, _____ I have to look it up	Espere que lo busco en la guía *ehspehreh keh loh booskoh ehn lah gheeah*
I can't find the word/the ___ sentence	No puedo encontrar la palabra/la frase *noh pwehdoh ehnkohntrahr lah pahlahbrah/lah frahseh*
How do you say _____ that in...?	¿Cómo se dice eso en...? *kohmoh seh deeteh ehstoh ehn...?*
How do you pronounce _____ that?	¿Cómo se pronuncia? *kohmoh seh prohnoonthyah?*

Conversation

3

May I introduce myself? ___	Permítame presentarme
	pehrmeetahmeh prehsehntahrmeh
My name's... ___	Me llamo...
	meh lyahmoh...
I'm... ___	Soy...
	soy...
What's your name? ___	¿Cómo se llama?
	kohmoh seh lyahmah?
May I introduce...? ___	Permítame presentarle a...
	pehrmeetahmeh prehsehntahrleh ah...
This is my wife/ ___ daughter/mother/ girlfriend	Esta es mi mujer/mi hija/mi madre/mi amiga
	ehstah ehs mee moo<u>h</u>ehr/mee eehah /mee mahdreh/mee ahmeegah
– my husband/son/ ___ father/boyfriend.	Este es mi marido/mi hijo/mi padre/mi amigo
	ehsteh ehs mee mahreedoh/mee eehoh/mee pahdreh/mee ahmeegoh
How do you do ___	Hola, mucho gusto
	ohlah, moochoh goostoh
Pleased to meet you ___	Encantado(a) (de conocerle)
	ehnkahntahdoh(ah) (deh kohnohthehrleh)
Where are you from? ___	¿De dónde es usted?
	deh dohndeh ehs oostehd?
I'm from ___ England/Scotland/ Ireland/Wales	Soy inglés/esa escocés/esa irlandés/esa galés/esa
	soy eenglehs/ehsah ehskohthehs/ehsah eerlahndehs/ehsah gahlehs/ ehsah
What city do you live in? ___	¿En qué ciudad vive?
	ehn keh thyoodahdh beebeh?
In..., It's near... ___	En...Eso está cerca de...
	ehn...ehsoh ehstah thehrkah deh...
Have you been here ___ long?	¿Hace mucho que está aquí?
	ahtheh moochoh keh ehstah ahkee?
A few days ___	Unos días
	oonohs deeahs
How long are you ___ staying here?	¿Cuánto tiempo piensa quedarse?
	kwahntoh tyehmpoh pyehnsah kehdahrseh?
We're (probably) ___ leaving tomorrow/ in two weeks	Nos iremos (probablemente) mañana/dentro de dos semanas
	nohs eerehmohs (prohbahblehmehnteh) mahnyahnah/dehntroh deh dohs sehmahnahs
Where are you staying? ___	¿Dónde se aloja?
	dohndeh seh ahloh<u>h</u>ah?
In a hotel/an apartment ___	En un hotel/apartamento
	ehn oon ohtehl/ahpahrtahmehntoh
On a camp site ___	En un camping
	ehn oon kahmpeen
With friends/relatives ___	En casa de amigos/parientes
	ehn kahsah deh ahmeegohs/pahryehntehs
Are you here on your ___ own/with your family?	¿Ha venido solo(a)/con su familia?
	ah behneedoh sohloh(ah)/kohn soo fahmeelyah?

I'm on my own _____	He venido solo(a)
	eh behneedoh sohloh(ah)
I'm with my _____ partner/wife/husband	con mi pareja/mujer/marido
	kohn mee pahrehhah/moohehr/mahreedoh
– with my family _____	con mi familia
	kohn mee fahmeelyah
– with relatives _____	con unos parientes
	kohn oonohs pahryehntehs
– with a friend/friends _____	con un amigo/una amiga/unos amigos
	kohn oon ahmeegoh/oonah ahmeegah/oonohs ahmeegohs
Are you married? _____	¿Está casado/casada?
	ehstah kahsahdoh/kahsahdah?
Do you have a steady boyfriend/girlfriend? _____	¿Tienes novio/novia?
	tyehnehs nohbyoh/nohbyah?
That's none of your business. _____	No es asunto suyo
	noh ehs ahsoontoh sooyoh
I'm married _____	Soy casado
	soy kahsahdoh
– single _____	Soy soltero
	soy sohltehroh
– separated _____	Estoy separado
	ehstoy sehpahrahdoh
– divorced _____	Estoy divorciado
	ehstoy deebohrthyahdoh
– a widow/widower _____	Soy viuda/viudo
	soy byoodah/byoodoh
I live alone/with someone _____	Vivo solo(a)/con otra persona
	beeboh sohloh(ah)/kohn ohtrah pehrsohnah
Do you have any children/grandchildren? _____	¿Tiene hijos/nietos?
	tyehneh eehohs/nyehtohs?
How old are you? _____	¿Cuántos años tiene?
	kwahntohs ahnyohs tyehneh?
How old is she/he? _____	¿Cuántos años tiene?
	kwahntohs ahnyohs tyehneh?
I'm... _____	Tengo...años
	tehngoh...ahnyohs
She's/he's... _____	Tiene...años
	tyehneh...ahnyohs
What do you do for a living? _____	¿En qué trabaja?
	ehn keh trahbahhah?
I work in an office _____	Trabajo en una oficina
	trahbahhoh ehn oonah ohfeetheenah
I'm a student/ I'm at school _____	Estudio
	ehstoodyoh
I'm unemployed _____	Estoy en paro
	ehstoy ehn pahroh
I'm retired _____	Soy jubilado
	soy hoobeelahdoh
I'm on a disability pension _____	Tengo una pensión de invalidez
	tehngoh oonah pehnsyohn deh eenbahleedeth
I'm a housewife _____	Soy ama de casa
	soy ahmah deh kahsah
Do you like your job? _____	¿Le gusta su trabajo?
	leh goostah soo trahbahhoh?

Most of the time _____	A veces sí, a veces no
	ah behtehs see, ah behtehs noh
I usually do, but I prefer ___ holidays	Por lo general sí, pero prefiero las vacaciones
	pohr loh hehnehrahl see, pehroh prehfyehroh lahs bahkahthyohnehs

3 .3 Starting/ending a conversation

Could I ask you _____ something?	¿Podría preguntarle una cosa?
	pohdreeah prehgoontahrleh oonah kohsah?
Excuse me	Perdone
	pehrdohneh
Excuse me, could you _____ help me?	¿Podría ayudarme?
	pohdreeah ahyoodahrmeh?
Yes, what's the problem? __	Sí, ¿qué pasa?
	see, keh pahsah?
What can I do for you? ____	¿En qué puedo servirle?
	ehn keh pwehdoh sehrbeerleh?
Sorry, I don't have time____ now	Lo siento, ahora no tengo tiempo
	loh syehntoh, ahohrah noh tehngoh tyehmpoh
Do you have a light? _____	¿Tiene fuego?
	tyehneh fwehgoh?
May I join you? _____	¿Le importa que me siente?
	leh eempohrtah keh meh syehnteh?
Could you take a _____ picture of me/us? Press this button.	¿Podría sacarme/sacarnos una foto? Hay que apretar este botón
	pohdreeah sahkahrmeh/sahkahrnohs oonah fohtoh? ay keh ahprehtahr ehsteh bohtohn
Leave me alone _____	Déjeme en paz
	dehhehmeh ehn pahth
Get lost_____	Váyase al diablo
	bahyahseh ahl deeahbloh
Go away or I'll scream_____	Como no se vaya, grito
	kohmoh noh seh bahyah, greetoh

3 .4 Congratulations and condolences

Happy birthday/many_____ happy returns	Feliz cumpleaños/felicidades
	fehleeth koomplehahnyohs/fehleetheedahdehs
Please accept my_____ condolences.	Le acompaño en el sentimiento
	leh ahkohmpahnyoh ehn ehl sehnteemyehntoh
I'm very sorry for you _____	¡Cuánto lo siento por usted!
	kwahntoh loh syehntoh pohr oostehdh!

3 .5 A chat about the weather

See also 1.5 The weather

It's so hot/cold today!_____	¡Qué calor/frío hace hoy!
	keh kahlohr/freeoh ahtheh oy!
Nice weather, isn't it? _____	¡Qué buen tiempo hace! ¿Verdad?
	keh bwehn tyehmpoh ahtheh! behrdah?

What a wind/storm! _____	¡Vaya viento/tormenta!
	bahyah byehntoh/tohrmentah!
All that rain/snow! _____	¡Cómo llueve/nieva!
	kohmoh lywehbeh/nyehbah!
All that fog! _____	¡Cuánta niebla!
	kwahntah nyehblah!
Has the weather been _____ like this for long here?	¿Hace mucho que hace este tiempo?
	ahteh moochoh keh ahteh ehsteh tyehmpoh?
Is it always this hot/cold ___ here?	¿Aquí siempre hace tanto calor/frío?
	ahkee syehmpreh ahteh tahntoh kahlohr/freeoh?
Is it always this dry/wet_____ here?	¿Aquí siempre hace un tiempo tan seco/lluvioso?
	ahkee syehmpreh ahteh oon tyehmpoh tahn sehkoh/lyoobyohsoh?

.6 Hobbies

Do you have any _____ hobbies?	¿Tiene algún hobby?
	tyehneh algoon <u>h</u>ohbee?
I like painting/_____ reading/photography/ DIY	Me gusta pintar/leer/la fotografía/el bricolaje
	meh goostah peentahr/lehehr/lah fohtohgrahfeeah/ehl breekohlah<u>h</u>eh
I like music _____	Me gusta la música
	meh goostah lah mooseekah
I like playing the _____ guitar/piano	Me gusta tocar la guitarra/el piano
	meh goostah tohkahr lah gueetahrrah/ehl pyahnoh
I like going to the movies __	Me gusta ir al cine
	meh goostah eer ahl theeneh
I like travelling/_____ sport/fishing/walking	Me gusta viajar/hacer deporte/pescar/salir a caminar
	meh goostah byah<u>h</u>ahr/ahtehr dehpohrteh/pehskahr/sahleer ah kahmeenahr

.7 Being the host(ess)

See also 4 Eating out

Can I offer you a drink? ____	¿Le gustaría algo de beber?
	leh goostahreeah ahlgoh deh behbehr?
What would you like_____ to drink?	¿Qué quieres beber?
	keh kyehrehs behbehr?
Something non-alcoholic,__ please.	Algo sin alcohol
	ahlgoh seen ahlkohl
Would you like a _____ cigarette/cigar/to roll your own?	¿Quiere un cigarrillo/un puro/liar un cigarrillo?
	kyehreh oon theegahrreelyoh/oon pooroh/leeahr oon theegahrreelyoh?
I don't smoke _____	No fumo
	noh foomoh

.8 Invitations

Are you doing anything tonight?	¿Tiene algo que hacer esta noche? *tyehneh ahlgoh keh ahtehehr ehstah nohcheh?*
Do you have any plans for today/this afternoon/tonight?	¿Ya tiene planes para hoy/esta tarde/esta noche? *yah tyehneh plahnehs pahrah oy/ehstah tahrdeh/ehstah nohcheh?*
Would you like to go out with me?	¿Le(te) apetece salir conmigo? *leh(teh) ahpehtehtheh sahleer kohnmeegoh?*
Would you like to go dancing with me?	¿Le(te) apetece ir a bailar conmigo? *leh(teh) ahpehtehtheh eer ah baylahr kohnmeegoh?*
Would you like to have lunch/dinner with me?	¿Le(te) apetece comer/cenar conmigo? *leh(teh) ahpehtehtheh kohmehr/thenahr kohnmeegoh?*
Would you like to come to the beach with me?	¿Le(te) apetece ir a la playa conmigo? *leh(teh) ahpehtehtheh eer ah lah plahyah kohnmeegoh?*
Would you like to come into town with us?	¿Le apetece ir a la ciudad con nosotros? *leh ahpehtehtheh eer ah lah thyoodahdh kohn nohsohtrohs?*
Would you like to come and see some friends with us?	¿Le apetece ir a casa de unos amigos con nosotros? *leh ahpehtehtheh eer ah kahsah deh oonohs ahmeegohs kohn nohsohtrohs?*
Shall we dance?	¿Bailamos? *baylahmohs?*
– sit at the bar?	¿Vienes a sentarte conmigo en la barra? *byehnehs ah sehntahrteh kohnmeegoh ehn lah bahrrah?*
– get something to drink?	¿Vamos a beber algo? *bahmohs ah behbehr ahlgoh?*
– go for a walk/drive?	¿Vamos a dar una vuelta? *bahmohs ah dahr oonah bwehltah?*
Yes, all right	Sí, vamos *see, bahmohs*
Good idea	Buena idea *bwehnah eedehah*
No (thank you)	No (gracias) *noh (grahthyahs)*
Maybe later	Quizá más tarde *keethah mahs tahrdeh*
I don't feel like it	No me apetece *noh meh ahpehtehtheh*
I don't have time	No tengo tiempo *noh tehngoh tyehmpoh*
I already have a date	Ya tengo otro compromiso *yah tehngoh ohtroh kohmprohmeesoh*
I'm not very good at dancing/volleyball/swimming	No sé bailar/jugar al vóleibol/nadar *noh seh baylahr/hoogahr ahl vohleheebohl/nahdahr*

3.9 Paying a compliment

You look wonderful! _____	¡Qué guapo/guapa está(estás)!
	keh wahpoh/wahpah ehstah(ehstahs)!
I like your car! _____	¡Qué bonito coche!
	keh bohneetoh kohcheh!
I like your ski outfit! _____	¡Qué bonito traje de esquiar!
	keh bohneetoh trah<u>h</u>eh deh ehskeeahr!
You're a nice boy/girl _____	Eres muy bueno/buena
	ehrehs mwee bwehnoh/bwehnah
What a sweet child! _____	¡Qué niño tan majo/niña tan maja!
	keh neenyoh tahn mah<u>h</u>oh/neenyah tahn
	mah<u>h</u>ah!
You're a wonderful _____ dancer!	Bailas muy bien
	bahylahs mwee byehn
You're a wonderful _____ cook!	Cocinas muy bien
	kohtheenahs mwee byehn
You're a terrific soccer _____ player!	Juegas muy bien al fútbol
	<u>h</u>wehgahs mwee byehn ahl footbohl

3.10 Chatting someone up

I like being with you _____	Me gusta estar contigo
	meh goostah ehstahr kohnteegoh
I've missed you so much __	Te he echado mucho de menos
	teh eh ehchahdoh moochoh deh mehnohs
I dreamt about you _____	He soñado contigo
	eh sohnyahdoh kohnteegoh
I think about you all day ___	Pienso todo el día en ti
	pyehnsoh tohdoh ehl deeah ehn tee
You have such a sweet _____ smile	Tienes una sonrisa muy bonita
	tyehnehs oonah sohnreesah mwee
	bohneetah
You have such beautiful ___ eyes	Tienes unos ojos muy bonitos
	tyehnehs oonohs oh<u>h</u>ohs mwee
	bohneetohs
I'm in love with you _____	Estoy enamorado/enamorada de ti
	ehstoy ehnahmohrahdoh/ehnahmohrahdah
	deh tee
I'm in love with you too ___	Yo también de ti
	yoh tahmbyehn deh tee
I love you_____	Te quiero
	teh kyehroh
I love you too _____	Yo también a ti
	yoh tahmbyehn ah tee
I don't feel as strongly _____ about you	Yo no siento lo mismo por ti
	yoh noh syehntoh loh meesmoh pohr tee
I already have a _____ boyfriend/girlfriend	Ya tengo pareja
	yah tehngoh pahreh<u>h</u>ah
I'm not ready for that_____	Yo no estoy preparado(a)
	yoh noh ehstoy prehpahrahdoh/ah
This is going too fast _____ for me	Vamos demasiado rápido
	bahmohs dehmahsyahdoh rahpeedoh
Take your hands off me_____	No me toque(s)
	noh meh tohkeh(s)
Okay, no problem _____	Vale, no importa
	bahleh, noh eempohrtah

Conversation

Conversation

Will you stay with me _____ ¿Te quedas a dormir?
tonight? *teh kehdahs ah dohrmeer?*

I'd like to go to bed_____ Me gustaría acostarme contigo
with you *meh goostahreeah ahkohstahrmeh*
kohnteegoh

Only if we use a condom _ Sólo si usamos condón
sohloh see oosahmohs kohndohn

We have to be careful _____ Hay que tener cuidado por lo del Sida
about AIDS *ay keh tehnehr kweedahdoh pohr loh dehl*
seedah

That's what they all say_____ Eso es lo que dicen todos
ehsoh ehs loh keh deethehn tohdohs

We shouldn't take any _____ Más vale no arriesgarse
risks *mahs bahleh noh ahrryehsgahrseh*

Do you have a condom? __ ¿Llevas condones?
lyehbahs kohndohnehs?

No? In that case we _____ ¿No? Pues entonces no
won't do it *noh? pwehs ehntohnthehs noh*

3.11 Arrangements

When will I see_____ ¿Cuándo te veo?
you again? *kwahndoh teh behoh?*

Are you free over the _____ ¿Tiene tiempo este fin de semana?
weekend? *tyehneh tyehmpoh ehsteh feen deh*
sehmahnah?

What shall we arrange?_____ ¿Cómo quedamos?
kohmoh kehdahmohs?

Where shall we meet? _____ ¿Dónde nos encontramos?
dohndeh nohs ehnkohntrahmohs?

Will you pick me/us up? __ ¿Me/nos pasa a buscar?
meh/nohs pahsah ah booskahr?

Shall I pick you up? _____ ¿Lo/la paso a buscar?
loh/lah pahsoh ah booskahr?

I have to be home by... _____ Tengo que estar en casa a las...
tehngoh keh ehstahr ehn kahsah ah lahs...

I don't want to see _____ No quiero volver a verlo/verla
you anymore *noh kyehroh bohlbehr ah behrloh/behrlah*

3.12 Saying goodbye

Can I take you home? _____ ¿Lo/la acompaño a su casa?
loh/lah ahkohmpahnyoh ah soo kahsah?

Can I write/call you? _____ ¿Puedo escribirle/llamarlo/llamarla por
teléfono?
pwehdoh ehskreebeerleh /lyahmahrloh/
lyahmahrlah pohr tehlehfohnoh?

Will you write/call me? _____ ¿Me escribirá/llamará por teléfono?
meh ehskreebeerah/lyahmahrah pohr
tehlehfohnoh?

Can I have your _____ ¿Me da su dirección/número de teléfono?
address/phone number? *meh dah soo deerehkthyohn/noomehroh deh*
tehlehfohnoh?

Thanks for everything _____ Gracias por todo
grahthyahs pohr tohdoh

It was very nice _____ Lo hemos pasado muy bien
loh ehmohs pahsahdoh mwee byehn

Say hello to...	Recuerdos a... *rehkwehrdohs ah...*
All the best	Te deseo lo mejor *teh dehsehoh loh meh<u>h</u>ohr*
Good luck	Que te vaya bien *keh teh bahyah byehn*
When will you be back?	¿Cuándo vuelves? *kwahndoh bwehlbehs?*
I'll be waiting for you	Te esperaré *teh ehspehrahreh.*
I'd like to see you again	Me gustaría volver a verte *meh goostahreeah bohlbehr ah behrteh*
I hope we meet again soon	Espero que nos volvamos a ver pronto *ehspehroh keh nohs bohlbahmohs ah behr prohntoh*
This is our address. If you're ever in the UK	Esta es nuestra dirección. Si alguna vez pasa por el Reino Unido... *ehstah ehs nwehstrah deerehkthyohn. see ahlgoonah behth pahsah pohr ehl reheenoh ooneedoh...*
You'd be more than welcome	Está cordialmente invitado *ehstah kohrdyahlmehnteh eenbeetahdoh*

3

Conversation

Eating out

Eating out

● **In Spain** people usually have three meals:
1 *El desayuno* (breakfast) approximately between 7 and 10 am.
Breakfast is light and consists of *café con leche* (white coffee), a
croissant or *suizo* (light sugary bun) or *tostadas* (toast).
2 *El almuerzo* (lunch) approx. between 2 and 4 pm, though hotels
usually serve at standard times. Lunch always includes a hot dish and
is the most important meal of the day. Office workers and
schoolchildren still lunch at home. It usually consists of four courses:
– starter (which can be a plate of greens)
– main course
– dessert
– fruit
3 *La cena* (dinner) between 9 and 11pm, 8pm in most hotels. Dinner is
usually a light, hot meal, taken with the family.
At around 6 or 7pm, a snack (*la merienda*) is often served, consisting
frequently of sandwiches with *chorizo* or *jamón serrano* and *pastas*
(biscuits) or small cakes.
Pinchos and *tapas* are often taken at bars with an apéritif, either in the
late morning or the evening.

4 .1 **O**n arrival

I'd like to book a table _____ for seven o'clock, please	¿Podría reservar una mesa para las siete? *pohdreeah rehsehrbahr oonah mehsah pahrah lahs syehteh?*
I'd like a table for two, _____ please	Quisiera una mesa para dos personas *keesyehrah oonah mehsah pahrah dohs pehrsohnahs*
We've/we haven't booked __	(No) hemos reservado *(noh) ehmohs rehsehrbahdoh*
Is the restaurant open _____ yet?	¿Ya está abierto el restaurante? *yah ehstah ahbyehrtoh ehl rehstahoorahnteh?*
What time does the _____ restaurant open/close?	¿A qué hora abre/cierra el restaurante? *ah keh ohrah ahbreh/thyehrrah ehl rehstahoorahnteh?*
Can we wait for a table? ___	¿Podemos esperar hasta que se desocupe una mesa? *pohdehmohs ehspehrahr ahstah keh seh dehsohkoopeh oonah mehsah?*
Do we have to wait long? __	¿Tenemos que esperar mucho? *tehnehmohs keh ehspehrahr moochoh?*

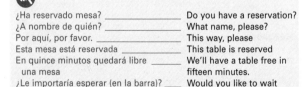

¿Ha reservado mesa? _____	Do you have a reservation?
¿A nombre de quién? _____	What name, please?
Por aquí, por favor. _____	This way, please
Esta mesa está reservada _____	This table is reserved
En quince minutos quedará libre _____ una mesa	We'll have a table free in fifteen minutes.
¿Le importaría esperar (en la barra)? ____	Would you like to wait (at the bar)?

Is this seat taken?	¿Está ocupada esta silla?
	ehstah ohkoopahdah ehstah seelyah?
Could we sit here/there?	¿Podemos sentarnos aquí/allí?
	pohdemohs sehntahrnohs ahkee/ahlyee?
Can we sit by the window?	¿Podemos sentarnos junto a la ventana?
	pohdehmohs sehntahrnohs hoontoh ah lah behntahnah?
Can we eat outside?	¿Podemos comer afuera?
	pohdehmohs kohmehr ahfwehrah?
Do you have another chair for us?	¿Podría traernos otra silla?
	pohdreeah trahehrnohs ohtrah seelyah?
Do you have a highchair?	¿Podría traernos una silla para niños?
	pohdreeah trahehrnohs oonah seelyah pahrah neenyohs?
Is there a socket for this bottle-warmer?	¿Hay un enchufe para este calentador de biberones?
	ay oon ehnchoofeh pahrah ehsteh kahlehntahdohr deh beebehrohnehs?
Could you warm up this bottle/jar for me?	¿Podría calentarme este biberón/este bote?
	pohdreeah kahlehntahrmeh ehsteh beebehrohn/ehsteh bohteh?
Not too hot, please	Que no esté muy caliente, por favor
	keh noh ehsteh mwee kahlyehnteh pohr fahbohr
Is there somewhere I can change the baby's nappy?	¿Hay algún lugar para cambiar al bebé?
	ay ahlgoon loogahr pahrah kahmbyahr ahl behbeh?
Where are the toilets?	¿Dónde están los servicios?
	dohnde ehstahn lohs sehrbeethyohs?

4.2 Ordering

Waiter!	¡Camarero!
	kahmahrehroh!
Madam!/Sir!	¡Oiga, (por favor)!
	oygah (pohr fahbohr)!
We'd like something to eat/a drink	Quisiéramos comer/beber algo
	keesyehrahmohs kohmehr/behber ahlgoh
Could I have a quick meal?	¿Podría comer algo rápido?
	pohdreeah kohmehr ahlgoh rahpeedoh?
We don't have much time	Tenemos poco tiempo
	tehnehmohs pohkoh tyehmpoh
We'd like to have a drink first	Antes quisiéramos beber algo
	ahntehs keesyehrahmohs behber ahlgoh
Could we see the menu/wine list, please?	¿Nos podría traer la carta/la carta de vinos?
	nohs pohdreeah trahehr lah kahrtah/lah kahrtah deh beenohs?
Do you have a menu in English?	¿Tienen menú en inglés?
	tyehnehn mehnoo ehn eenglehs?
Do you have a dish of the day?	¿Tienen menú del día/menú turístico?
	tyehnehn mehnoo dehl deeah/mehnoo tooreesteekoh?
We haven't made a choice yet	Todavía no hemos elegido
	tohdahbeeah noh ehmohs ehlehheedoh

What do you recommend?	¿Qué nos recomienda?
	keh nohs rehkohmyehndah?
What are the specialities of the region/the house?	¿Cuáles son las especialidades de la región/de la casa?
	kwahlehs sohn lahs ehspehthyahleedahdehs deh lah reh<u>h</u>yohn/deh lah kahsah?
I like strawberries/olives	Me gustan las fresas/las aceitunas
	meh goostahn lahs frehsahs/lahs ahtheheetoonahs
I don't like meat/fish/...	No me gusta el pescado/la carne/...
	noh meh goostah ehl pehskahdoh/lah kahrneh/...
What's this?	¿Qué es esto?
	keh ehs ehstoh?
Does it have...in it?	¿Lleva...?
	lyehbah...?
What does it taste like?	¿A qué sabe?
	ah keh sahbeh?
Is this a hot or a cold dish?	¿Es un plato caliente o frío?
	ehs oon plahtoh kahlyehnteh oh freeoh?
Is this sweet?	¿Es un plato dulce?
	ehs oon plahtoh doolthe?
Is this spicy?	¿Es un plato picante?
	ehs oon plahtoh peekahnteh?
Do you have anything else, please?	¿Tendría otra cosa?
	tehndreeah ohtrah kohsah?
I'm on a salt-free diet	No puedo comer sal
	noh pwehdoh kohmehr sahl
I can't eat pork	No puedo comer carne de cerdo
	noh pwehdoh kohmehr kahrneh deh thehrdoh
– sugar	No puedo comer azúcar
	noh pwehdo kohmehr ahthookahr
– fatty foods	No puedo comer grasa
	noh pwehdoh kohmehr grahsah
– (hot) spices	No puedo comer cosas picantes
	noh pwehdoh kohmehr kohsahs peekahntehs
I'll/we'll have what those people are having	Lo mismo que esos señores, por favor
	loh meesmoh keh ehsohs sehnyohrehs pohr fahbohr

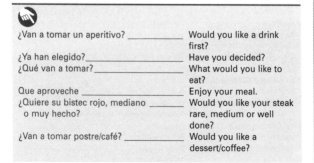

¿Van a tomar un aperitivo?	Would you like a drink first?
¿Ya han elegido?	Have you decided?
¿Qué van a tomar?	What would you like to eat?
Que aproveche	Enjoy your meal.
¿Quiere su bistec rojo, mediano o muy hecho?	Would you like your steak rare, medium or well done?
¿Van a tomar postre/café?	Would you like a dessert/coffee?

I'd like...	Para mí...
	pahrah mee...
We're not having a starter	No vamos a comer primer plato
	noh bahmohs ah kohmehr preemehr plahtoh
The child will share what we're having	El niño/la niña comerá de nuestro menú
	ehl neenyoh/lah neenyah kohmehrah deh
	nwehstroh mehnoo
Could I have some more bread, please?	Más pan, por favor
	mahs pahn pohr fahbohr
– a bottle of water/wine	Otra botella de agua/de vino, por favor
	ohtrah bohtehllyah deh ahgwah/deh beenoh,
	pohr fahbohr
– another helping of...	Otra ración de..., por favor
	ohtrah rahthyohn deh..., pohr fahbohr
– some salt and pepper	¿Podría traerme sal y pimienta?
	pohdreeah trahehrmeh sahl ee
	peemyehntah?
– a napkin	¿Podría traerme una servilleta?
	pohdreeah trahehrmeh oonah
	sehrbeellyehtah?
– a spoon	¿Podría traerme una cuchara?
	pohdreeah trahehrmeh oonah koochahrah?
– an ashtray	¿Podría traerme un cenicero?
	pohdreeah trahehrmeh oon thehneethehroh?
– some matches	¿Podría traerme unas cerillas?
	pohdreeah trahehrmeh oonahs
	thehreellyahs?
– some toothpicks	¿Podría traerme unos palillos?
	pohdreeah trahehrmeh oonohs pahleellyohs?
– a glass of water	¿Podría traerme un vaso de agua?
	pohdreeah trahehrmeh oon bahsoh deh
	ahgwah?
– a straw (for the child)	¿Podría traerme una pajita (para el niño/
	la niña)?
	pohdreeah trahehrmeh oonah pahheetah
	(pahrah ehl neenyoh/lah neenyah)?
Enjoy your meal!	¡Que aproveche!
	keh ahprohbehcheh!
You too!	Igualmente
	eegwahlmehnteh
Cheers!	¡Salud!
	sahloodh!
The next round's on me	La próxima ronda la pago yo
	lah prohxeemah rohndah lah pahgoh yoh
Could we have a doggy bag, please?	¿Podemos llevarnos las sobras?
	pohdehmohs lyehbarnohs lahs sohbrahs?

4 .3 The bill

See also 8.2 Settling the bill

How much is this dish?	¿Cuánto vale este plato?
	kwahntoh bahleh ehsteh plahtoh?
Could I have the bill, please?	La cuenta, por favor
	lah kwehntah, pohr fahbohr
All together	Todo junto
	tohdoh hoontoh

Everyone pays separately __	Cada uno paga lo suyo
	kahdah oonoh pahgah loh sooyoh
Could we have the menu __ again, please?	¿Podría traernos otra vez la carta?
	pohdreeah trahehrnohs ohtrah behth lah kahrtah?
The...is not on the bill ____	Ha olvidado apuntar el/la...
	ah olbeedahdoh ahpoontahr ehl/lah...

.4 Complaints

It's taking a very long time	Están tardando mucho
	ehstahn tahrdahndoh moochoh
We've been here an hour already	Ya llevamos una hora aquí
	yah lyebahmohs oonah ohrah ahkee
This must be a mistake ____	Esto tiene que ser una equivocación
	ehstoh tyehneh keh sehr oonah ehkeebohkahthyohn
This is not what I ordered	Esto no es lo que he pedido
	ehstoh noh ehs loh keh eh pehdeedoh
I ordered... ____	He pedido...
	eh pehdeedoh
There's a dish missing ____	Falta un plato
	fahltah oon plahtoh
This is broken/not clean ___	Esto está roto/no está limpio
	ehstoh ehstah rohtoh/noh ehstah leempyoh
The food's cold ____	La comida está fría
	lah kohmeedah ehstah freeah
– not fresh ____	La comida no es fresca
	lah kohmeedah noh ehs frehskah
– too salty/sweet/spicy ____	La comida está muy salada/dulce/picante
	lah kohmeedah ehstah mwee sahlahdah/dooltheh/peekahnteh
The meat's not done ____	La carne está cruda
	lah kahrneh ehstah kroodah
– overdone ____	La carne está muy hecha
	lah kahrneh ehstah mwee ehchah
– tough ____	La carne está dura
	lah kahrneh ehstah doorah
– off ____	La carne está podrida
	lah kahrneh ehstah pohdreedah
Could I have something else instead of this?	¿Me podría traer otra cosa en lugar de esto?
	meh pohdreeah trahehr ohtrah kohsah ehn loogahr deh ehstoh?
The bill/this amount is not right	La cuenta/este precio está mal
	lah kwehntah/ehsteh prehthyoh ehstah mahl
We didn't have this ____	Esto no lo hemos comido/bebido
	ehstoh noh loh ehmohs kohmeedoh/behbeedoh
There's no paper in the toilet	No hay papel en el servicio
	noh ay pahpehl ehn ehl sehrbeethyoh
Do you have a complaints book?	¿Tienen libro de quejas?
	tyehnen leebroh deh kehhas?
Will you call the manager, please?	Haga el favor de llamar al jefe
	ahgah ehl fahbohr deh lyamahr ahl hehfeh

.5 Paying a compliment

That was a wonderful meal _____	Hemos comido muy bien *ehmohs kohmeedoh mwee byehn*
The food was excellent _____	La comida ha estado exquisita *lah kohmeedah ah ehstahdoh ehxkeeseetah*
The...in particular was _____ delicious	Sobre todo nos ha gustado el/la... *sohbreh tohdoh nohs ah goostahdoh ehl/lah...*

.6 The menu

aperitivo apéritif	mariscos seafood	postres sweets/dessert
aves poultry	pastelería pastry	primeros platos starters
azúcar sugar	pescados fish	raciones portions
bebidas alcohólicas alcoholic beverages	platos calientes hot dishes	servicio incluido service included
bebidas calientes hot beverages	platos combinados combined dishes	sopas soups
carta de vinos wine list	plato del día dish of the day	tapas tapas
cócteles cocktails	platos fríos cold dishes	venado game
cubierto cover charge	platos principales main courses	verduras vegetables
entremeses variados hors d'oeuvres	platos típicos regional specialities	

.7 Alphabetical list of drinks and dishes

aceituna olive	anís aniseed	biftec steak
aguacate avocado	apio celery	bizcocho (borracho) sponge cake(with sherry or similar)
ajo garlic	arenque herring	bocadillo sandwich
albóndigas meat balls	arroz rice	buey/vaca beef
alcachofa artichoke	asado roast, roasted	cabrito kid
almejas clams	atún/bonito tuna	café (solo/con leche) coffee (black/white)
almendras almonds	avellana hazelnut	calamares (en su tinta)
ancas de rana frog's legs	bacalao cod	squid (cooked in their ink)
anchoa/boquerón anchovy	batido de... ...milk shake	caldo broth
anguila eel	berenjena aubergine	callos tripe

cangrejo	criadillas/mollejas	grosellas
crab	sweetbreads	red/black currants
caracoles	crudo	guisado
snails	raw	stew
carne	cuba libre	guisantes
meat	rum coke	peas
carpa	dátil	habas
carp	date	broad beans
castaña	dulce	harina
chestnut	sweet	flour
cebolla	emperador	hígado de oca
onion	swordfish	goose liver
cerdo	en escabeche	higo
pork	pickled	fig
cerezas	endibia	huevos al plato/ duros/revueltos
cherries	chicory/endive	fried/hard boiled/scrambled eggs
cerveza	ensalada (mixta)	
beer	mixed salad	jamón de York/serrano
chorizo	ensaladilla rusa	ham (cooked/Parma style)
chorizo (paprika flavoured salami sausage)	Russian salad	
	escalope	jerez (seco, dulce)
chucrut	escalope	sherry (dry, sweet)
sauerkraut	espárragos	judías verdes
chuleta/costilla	asparagus	French beans
chop	especies	jugo/zumo
churros	spices	fruit juice
fritters	espinaca	langosta
ciervo	spinach	lobster
venison	fideos	langostino
cigalas	noodles	crayfish
Dublin Bay prawns	filete	leche
ciruela	fillet	milk
plum	flan	lechuga
cochinillo asado	cream caramel	lettuce
roast suckling pig	frambuesa	legumbres
cocido	raspberry	vegetables (legumes)
boiled	fresa	lengua
codorniz	strawberry	tongue
quail	frito	lenguado
col/berza	fried	sole
cabbage	fruta (del tiempo)	lentejas
coles de Bruselas	seasonal fruit	lentils
Brussels sprouts	galleta	licor
coliflor	biscuit	liqueur
cauliflower	gambas	liebre
coñac	prawns	hare
brandy	garbanzos	limón
conejo	chick peas	lemon
rabbit	gazpacho andaluz	lomo de cerdo
copa helada/helado	gazpacho (cold soup)	tenderloin of pork
ice cream	granizado de limón/café	
cordero	iced drink (lemon/coffee)	
lamb		
crema/nata		
cream		

maíz (mazorca)
corn (on the cob)
mantequilla
butter
manzana
apple
mazapán
marzipan
mejillones
mussels
melocotón (en
  almíbar)
peach (in syrup)
melón
melon
membrillo
quince
merluza
hake
mermelada
jam
mero
sea bass
morcilla
black pudding
mostaza
mustard
muslo de pollo
drumstick
nuez
walnut
ostras
oysters
paella
paella
pan
bread
pastel
cake
patatas fritas
chips/crisps
pato (silvestre)
(wild) duck
pechuga (de pollo)
(chicken) breast
pepino
cucumber
pepinillos
gherkins
pera
pear

perdiz
partridge
perejil
parsley
pescado
fish
picadillo de ternera
minced veal
pierna (de cordero)
leg (of lamb)
pimentón
paprika
pimienta
pepper
pimientos
green/red peppers
piña
pineapple
plancha (a la)
grilled
plátano
banana
plato principal
main course
platos típicos
regional specialities
pollo
chicken
puerro
leek
pulpo
octopus
queso
cheese
rábanos
radishes
rabo de buey
oxtail
rape
monkfish
remolacha
beetroot
riñones
kidneys
rodaballo
turbot
romana (a la)
deep fried
vino rosado
rosé wine
salchicha
sausage

salchichón
salami
salmón
salmon
salmón ahumado
smoked salmon
salmonete
red mullet
sandía
water melon
sangría
sangría
sardinas
sardines
setas
mushrooms
solomillo de buey
fillet of beef
sopa
soup
tarta helada
ice cream cake
ternera
veal
tinto
red wine
tocino
bacon
tortilla española
Spanish omelette
  (potato)
tortilla francesa
plain omelette
tortitas
waffles
trucha
trout
trufas
truffles
turrón
nougat
uvas
grapes
verduras
green vegetables
vinagre
vinegar
zanahorias
carrots
zumo de naranja
orange juice

On the road

5.1 Asking for directions

Excuse me, could I ask you something?	Perdone, ¿podría preguntarle algo? *pehrdohneh, pohdreeah prehgoontahrleh ahlgoh?*
I've lost my way	Me he perdido *meh eh pehrdeedoh*
Is there a(n)... around here?	¿Sabe dónde hay un(a)...por aquí? *sahbeh dohndeh ay oon(ah)...pohr ahkee?*
Is this the way to...?	¿Se va por aquí a...? *seh bah pohr ahkee ah...?*
Could you tell me how to get to the... (name of place) by car/on foot?	¿Podría decirme cómo llegar a... (en coche/a pie)? *pohdreeah dehtheermeh kohmoh lyehgahr ah... (ehn kohcheh/ah pyeh)?*
What's the quickest way to...?	¿Cómo hago para llegar lo antes posible a...? *kohmoh ahgoh pahrah lyehgahr loh ahntehs pohseebleh ah...?*
How many kilometres is it to...?	¿Cuántos kilómetros faltan para llegar a...? *kwahntohs keelohmehtrohs fahltahn pahrah lyehgahr ah...?*
Could you point it out on the map?	¿Podría señalarlo en el mapa? *pohdreeah sehnyahlahrloh ehn ehl mahpah?*

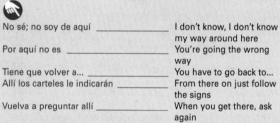

No sé; no soy de aquí	I don't know, I don't know my way around here
Por aquí no es	You're going the wrong way
Tiene que volver a...	You have to go back to...
Allí los carteles le indicarán	From there on just follow the signs
Vuelva a preguntar allí	When you get there, ask again

todo recto	la calle	el viaducto
straight ahead	the street	the fly-over
a la izquierda	el semáforo	el puente
left	the traffic light	the bridge
a la derecha	el túnel	el paso a nivel/las
right	the tunnel	barreras
doblar	el stop	the level
turn	the `give way' sign	crossing/the boom
seguir	el edificio	gates
follow	the building	el cartel en
cruzar	en la esquina	dirección de...
cross	at the corner	the sign pointing to...
el cruce	el río	la flecha
the intersection	the river	the arrow

5 .2 Customs

● **Border documents**: valid passport, visa. For car and motorbike: valid UK driving licence and registration document, insurance document, green card, UK registration plate.
Import and export specifications:
– Foreign currency: no restrictions
– Alcohol: 10 litres of spirits and 90 litres of wine. Tobacco: 800 cigarettes, 200 cigars or a kilo of tobacco. Restricted to personal consumption only.

Su pasaporte, por favor _____	Your passport, please
La tarjeta verde, por favor _____	Your green card, please
El permiso de circulación/la carta gris, por favor _____	Your vehicle documents, please
¿Adónde va? _____	Where are you heading?
¿Cuánto tiempo piensa quedarse? _____	How long are you planning to stay?
¿Tiene algo que declarar? _____	Do you have anything to declare?
¿Puede abrir esto? _____	Open this, please

My children are entered ___ on this passport	Mis hijos están apuntados en este pasaporte
	mees eehohs ehstahn ahpoontahdohs ehn ehsteh pahsahpohrteh
I'm travelling through _____	Estoy de paso
	ehstoy deh pahsoh
I'm going on holiday to... __	Voy de vacaciones a...
	boy deh bahkahthyohnehs ah...
I'm on a business trip _____	He venido en viaje de negocios
	eh behneedoh ehn byahheh deh nehgohthyohs
I don't know how long_____ I'll be staying yet	Todavía no sé cuánto tiempo me quedaré
	tohdahbeeah noh seh kwahntoh tyehmpoh meh kehdahreh
I'll be staying here for _____ a weekend	Pienso quedarme un fin de semana
	pyehnsoh kehdahrmeh oon feen deh sehmahnah
– for a few days _____	Pienso quedarme unos días
	pyehnsoh kehdahrmeh oonohs deeahs
– for a week_____	Pienso quedarme una semana
	pyehnsoh kehdahrmeh oonah sehmahnah
– for two weeks _____	Pienso quedarme dos semanas
	pyehnsoh kehdahrmeh dohs sehmahnahs
I've got nothing to_____ declare	No tengo nada que declarar
	noh tehngoh nahdah keh dehklahrahr
I've got...with me_____	Traigo...
	trahygoh...
– ...cartons of cigarettes ___	Traigo...cartones de cigarrillos
	trahygoh...kahrtohnehs deh theegahrreelyohs
– ...bottles of... _____	Traigo...botellas de...
	trahygoh...bohtehlyahs deh...

– some souvenirs _____	Traigo algunos recuerdos de viaje *trahygoh ahlgoonohs rehkwehrdohs de* *byahheh*
These are personal _____ effects	Estos son artículos personales *ehstohs sohn ahrteekooloohs pehrsohnahlehs*
These are not new _____	Estas cosas no son nuevas *ehstahs kohsahs noh sohn nwehbahs*
Here's the receipt _____	Aquí está el recibo *ahkee ehstah ehl rehtheeboh*
This is for private use _____	Esto es para uso personal *ehstoh ehs pahrah oosoh pehrsohnahl*
How much import duty _____ do I have to pay?	¿Cuánto tengo que pagar por derechos de aduana? *kwahntoh tehngoh keh pahgahr pohr* *dehrehchohs deh ahdwahnah?*
Can I go now? _____	¿Puedo seguir? *pwehdoh sehgheer?*

5 .3 Luggage

Porter! _____	¡Mozo! *mohthoh!*
Could you take this _____ luggage to...?	¿Podría llevar este equipaje a...? *pohdreeah lyehbahr ehsteh ehkeepahheh* *ah...?*
How much do I _____ owe you?	¿Cuánto le debo? *kwahntoh leh dehboh?*
Where can I find a _____ luggage trolley?	¿Dónde hay carritos para el equipaje? *dohndeh ay kahrreetohs pahrah ehl* *ehkeepahheh?*
Could you store this _____ luggage for me?	¿Podría dejar este equipaje en la consigna? *pohdreeah dehhahr ehsteh ehkeepahheh* *ehn lah kohnseegnah?*
Where are the luggage _____ lockers?	¿Dónde está la consigna automática? *dohndeh ehstah lah kohnseegnah* *ahootohmahteekah?*
I can't get the locker _____ open	No logro abrir la puerta de la consigna *noh lohgroh ahbreer lah pwehrtah deh lah* *kohnseegnah*
How much is it per item ___ per day?	¿Cuánto sale por bulto y por día? *kwahntoh sahleh pohr booltoh ee pohr* *deeah?*
This is not my bag/ _____ suitcase	Este/ésta no es mi bolso/mi maleta *ehsteh/ehstah noh ehs mee bohlsoh/mee* *mahlehtah*
There's one item/bag/ _____ suitcase missing still	Todavía falta un bulto/un bolso/una maleta *tohdahbeeah fahltah oon booltoh/oon* *bohlsoh/oonah mahlehtah*
My suitcase is damaged ___	Me han dañado la maleta *meh ahn dahnyahdoh lah mahlehtah*

🅢.4 Traffic signs

a la derecha right	ceda el paso give way	obras roadworks ahead
a la izquierda left	cerrado closed	paso a nivel (sin barreras) level crossing
abierto open	cruce peligroso dangerous crossing	(no gates)
altura máxima maximum height	curvas en ... km bends for...km	paso de ganado cattle crossing
arcenes sin afirmar soft verges	despacio drive slowly	peaje toll
¡atención, peligro! danger	desprendimientos loose rocks	peatones pedestrian crossing
autopista de peaje toll road	desvío diversion	precaución caution
autovía motorway	dirección prohibida no entry	prohibido aparcar no parking
bajada peligrosa steep hill	dirección única one-way traffic	prohibido adelantar no overtaking
calzada resbaladiza slippery road	encender las luces switch on lights	puesto de socorro first aid
cambio de sentido change of direction	espere wait	salida exit
cañada animals crossing	estacionamiento reglamentado limited parking zone	salida de camiones factory/works exit
carretera comarcal secondary road	excepto... except for...	substancias peligrosas dangerous substances
carretera cortada road closed	fin de... end of...	
carretera en mal estado irregular road surface	hielo ice on road	travesía peligrosa dangerous crossing
carretera nacional main road	niebla beware fog	zona peatonal pedestrian zone

🅢.5 The car

See the diagram on page 51.

● **The motorways in Spain** have been very well updated and expanded. Tolls, however, can be expensive.

Particular traffic regulations:
maximum speed for cars:
120km/h on toll roads
110km/h on other motorways
60km/h in town centres
– give way: all traffic from the right has the right of way, except for major roads and thoroughfares.
– towing: prohibited to private drivers.

On the road

5 .6 The petrol station

● **Petrol is easily available** but rather expensive in Spain.

How many kilometres to ___ the next petrol station, please?	¿Cuántos kilómetros faltan para la próxima gasolinera?
	kwahntohs keelohmehtrohs fahltahn pahrah lah prohxeemah gahsohleenehrah?
I would like...litres of..., ___ please	Póngame...litros de..., por favor
	pohngahmeh...leetrohs deh..., pohr fahbohr
– super ___	Póngame...litros de gasolina súper
	pohngahmeh...leetrohs de gahsohleenah soopehr
– leaded ___	Póngame...litros de gasolina normal
	pohngahmeh...leetrohs deh gahsohleenah nohrmahl
– unleaded ___	Póngame...litros de gasolina sin plomo
	pohngahmeh...leetrohs deh gahsohleenah seen plohmoh
– diesel ___	Póngame...litros de gasóleo
	pohngahmeh...leetrohs deh gahsohlehoh
I would like...pesetas' ___ worth of petrol, please	Póngame gasolina por...pesetas
	pohngahmeh gahsohleenah pohr...pehsehtahs
Fill her up, please ___	Lléneme el depósito, por favor
	lyehnehmeh ehl dehpohseetoh, pohr fahvohr
Could you check...? ___	¿Podría controlar...?
	pohdreeah kohntrohlahr?
– the oil level ___	¿Podría controlar el nivel del aceite?
	pohdreeah kohntrohlahr ehl neebehl dehl ahtheheeteh?
– the tyre pressure ___	¿Podría controlar la presión de los neumáticos?
	pohdreeah kohntrohlahr lah prehsyohn deh lohs nehoomahteekohs?
Could you change the ___ oil, please?	¿Podría cambiar el aceite?
	pohdreeah kahmbyahr ehl atheheeteh?
Could you clean the ___ windows/the windscreen, please?	¿Podría limpiar los cristales/el parabrisas?
	pohdreeah leempyahr lohs kreestahlehs/ehl pahrahbreesahs?
Could you give the car ___ a wash, please?	¿Podría lavar el coche?
	pohdreeah lahbahr ehl kohcheh?

On the road

I'm having car trouble.____ Tengo una avería. ¿Podría ayudarme?
Could you give me a _tehngoh oonah ahbehreeah. pohdreeah_
hand? _ahyoodahrmeh?_

I've run out of petrol _____ Me he quedado sin gasolina
meh eh kehdahdoh seen gahsohleenah

I've locked the keys_____ Me he dejado las llaves en el coche
in the car _meh eh deh_h_ahdoh lahs lyabehs ehn ehl_
kohcheh

The car/motorbike/ _____ El coche/la moto/el ciclomotor no arranca
moped won't start _ehl kohcheh/lah mohtoh/ehl_
theeklohmohtohr noh ahrrahnkah

Could you contact the _____ ¿Podría avisar al auxilio en carretera?
recovery service for me, _pohdreeah ahbeesar ahl ahooxeelyoh ehn_
please? _kahrrehtehrah?_

Could you call a garage____ ¿Podría llamar por teléfono a un taller
for me, please? mecánico?
pohdreeah lyahmahr pohr tehlehfohnoh ah
oon tahlyehr mehkahneekoh?

Could you give me _____ ¿Me podría llevar a...?
a lift to...? _meh pohdreeah lyehbahr ah...?_

– a garage/into town?_____ ¿Me podría llevar a un taller mecánico/a la
ciudad?
meh pohdreeah lyehbahr ah oon tahlyehr
mehkahneekoh/ah lah thyoodahdh?

– a phone booth?_____ ¿Me podría llevar a una cabina de
teléfonos?
meh pohdreeah lyehbahr ah oonah
kahbeenah deh tehlehfohnohs?

– an emergency phone? ___ ¿Me podría llevar a un teléfono de
emergencia?
meh pohdreeah lyehbahr ah oon
_tehlehfohnoh deh ehmehr_h_ehnthyah?_

Can we take my_____ ¿Podríamos llevar la bicicleta/el
bicycle/moped? ciclomotor?
pohdreeahmohs lyehbahr lah
beetheeklehtah/ehl theeklohmohtohr?

Could you tow me to _____ ¿Podría remolcarme hasta un taller
a garage? mecánico?
pohdreeah rehmohlkahrmeh ahstah oon
tahlyehr mehkahneekoh?

There's probably _____ Me parece que está fallando el/la...
something wrong _meh pahrehtheh keh ehstah fahlyahndoh_
with...(See 5.8). _ehl/lah..._

Can you fix it? _____ ¿Podría arreglarlo?
pohdreeah ahrrehglahrloh?

Could you fix my tyre? ____ ¿Podría arreglar el neumático?
pohdreeah ahrrehglahr ehl
nehoomahteekoh?

Could you change this_____ ¿Podría cambiar esta rueda?
wheel? _pohdreeah kahmbyahr ehstah_
rwehdah?

The parts of a car
(the diagram shows the numbered parts)

1 battery	la batería	*lah bahtehreeah*
2 rear light	el faro piloto	*ehl fahroh peelohtoh*
3 rear-view mirror	el retrovisor	*ehl rehtrohbeesohr*
reversing light	la luz de marcha atrás	*lah looth deh mahrchah ahtrahs*
4 aerial	la antena	*lah ahntehnah*
car radio	la autorradio	*lah ahootohrrahdyoh*
5 petrol tank	el depósito de gasolina	*ehl dehpohseetoh deh gahsohleenah*
inside mirror	el espejo interior	*ehl ehspehhoh eentehreeohr*
6 sparking plugs	las bujías	*lahs boo-heeahs*
fuel filter/pump	el separador de gasolina	*ehl sehpahrahdohr deh gahsohleenah*
7 wing mirror	el espejo exterior	*ehl ehspehoh ehxtehryohr*
8 bumper	el parachoques	*ehl pahrahchohkehs*
carburettor	el carburador	*ehl kahrboorahdohr*
crankcase	el cárter	*ehl kahrtehr*
cylinder	el cilindro	*ehl theeleendroh*
ignition	los contactos del ruptor	*lohs kohntahktohs dehl rooptohr*
warning light	la luz piloto	*lah looth peelohtoh*
dynamo	la dinamo	*lah deenahmoh*
accelerator	el pedal del acelerador	*ehl pehdahl dehl ahthehlehrahdohr*
handbrake	el freno de mano	*ehl frehnoh deh mahnoh*
valve	la válvula	*lah bahlboolah*
9 silencer	el silenciador	*ehl seelehnthyahdohr*
10 boot	el maletero	*ehl mahlehtehroh*
11 headlight	el faro	*ehl fahroh*
crank shaft	el cigueñal	*ehl theegwehnyahl*
12 air filter	el filtro de aire	*ehl feeltroh deh ayreh*
fog lamp	la luz antiniebla trasera	*lah looth ahnteenyehblah trahsehrah*
13 engine block	el bloque motor	*ehl blohkeh mohtohr*
camshaft	el árbol de levas	*ehl ahrbohl deh lehbahs*
oil filter/pump	el filtro de aceite	*ehl feeltroh deh ahtheheeteh*
dipstick	la varilla indicadora de nivel de aceite	*lah bahreelyah eendeekahdohrah deh neebehl deh ahtheyteh*
pedal	el pedal	*ehl pehdahl*
14 door	la portezuela	*lah pohrtehthwehlah*
15 radiator	el radiador	*ehl rahdyahdohr*
16 brake disc	el disco del freno	*ehl deeskoh dehl frehnoh*
spare wheel	la rueda de reserva	*lah rwehdah deh rehsehrbah*
17 indicator	el intermitente	*ehl eentehrmeetehnteh*
steering wheel	el volante	*ehl bohlahnteh*
18 windscreen wiper	el limpiaparabrisas	*ehl leempyahpahrahbreesahs*
19 shock absorbers	los amortiguadores	*lohs ahmohrteegwahdohrehs*
sunroof	el techo corredizo	*ehl tehchoh kohrrehdeethoh*
spoiler	el spoiler	*ehl spoheelehr*
starter motor	el motor de arranque	*ehl mohtohr deh ahrrahnkeh*

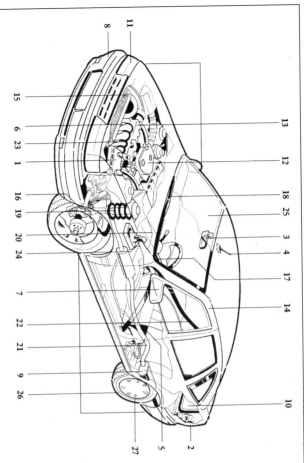

20 steering column	el cárter de la dirección	*ehl kahrtehr deh lah deerehkthyohn*
21 exhaust pipe	el tubo de escape	*ehl tooboh deh ehskahpeh*
22 seat belt	el cinturón de seguridad	*ehl theentoorohn deh sehgooreedahdh*
fan	el ventilador	*ehl behnteelahdohr*
23 distributor cables	los cables del distribuidor	*lohs kahblehs dehl deestreebweedohr*
24 gear lever	la palanca de cambios	*lah pahlahnkah deh kahmbyohs*
25 windscreen	el parabrisas	*ehl pahrahbreesahs*
water pump	la bomba de agua	*lah bohmbah deh ahgwah*
26 wheel	la rueda	*lah rwehdah*
27 hubcap	el tapacubos	*ehl tahpahkoobohs*
piston	el émbolo	*ehl ehmbohloh*

Can you fix it so it'll get me to...?	¿Podría arreglarlo de tal manera que pueda seguir hasta...?
	pohdreeah ahrrehglahrloh deh tahl mahnehrah keh pwehdah sehgheer ahstah...?
Which garage can help me?	¿En qué taller me podrán ayudar entonces?
	ehn keh tahlyehr meh pohdrahn ahyoodahr ehntohnthehs?
When will my car/bicycle be ready?	¿Para cuándo estará mi coche/bicicleta?
	pahrah kwahndoh ehstahrah mee kohcheh/beetheeklehtah?
Can I wait for it here?	¿Puedo esperar aquí?
	pwehdoh ehspehrahr ahkee?
How much will it cost?	¿Por cuánto me va a salir?
	pohr kwahntoh meh bah ah sahleer?
Could you itemise the bill?	¿Podría especificar la cuenta?
	pohdreeah ehspehtheefeekahr lah kwehntah?
Can I have a receipt for the insurance?	¿Me podría dar un recibo para el seguro?
	meh pohdreeah dahr oon rehtheeboh pahrah ehl sehgooroh?

.8 The bicycle/moped

See the diagram on page 55.

● **Cycle paths** are rare in Spain. Not much consideration for bikes should be expected on the roads. The maximum speed for mopeds is 40km/h both inside and outside town centres. A helmet is compulsory.

No tengo piezas de recambio para su coche/su bicicleta	I don't have parts for your car/bicycle
Las piezas de recambio me las tienen que traer de otro sitio	I have to get the parts from somewhere else
Las piezas de recambio tengo que encargarlas	I have to order the parts
Eso llevará medio día	That'll take half a day
Eso llevará un día	That'll take a day
Eso llevará unos días	That'll take a few days
Eso llevará una semana	That'll take a week
Su coche ha quedado totalmente destruido	Your car is a write-off
Ya no se puede hacer nada para arreglarlo	It can't be repaired
El coche/la moto/el ciclomotor/la bicicleta estará para las...	The car/motor bike/moped/bicycle will be ready at... o'clock

I'd like to rent a...	Quisiera alquilar un...
	keesyehrah ahlkeelahr oon...
Do I need a (special) licence for that?	¿Hace falta un permiso de conducir (especial)?
	ahtheh fahltah oon pehrmeesoh deh kohndootheer (ehspehthyahl)?
I'd like to rent the...for...	Quisiera alquilar el/la...por...
	keesyehrah ahlkeelahr ehl/lah...pohr...
– one day	Quisiera alquilar el/la...por un día
	keesyehrah ahlkeelahr ehl/lah...pohr oon deeah
– two days	Quisiera alquilar el/la...por dos días
	keesyehrah ahlkeelahr ehl/lah...pohr dohs deeahs
How much is that per day/week?	¿Cuánto sale por día/semana?
	kwahntoh sahleh pohr deeah/pohr sehmahnah?
How much is the deposit?	¿Cuánto es la fianza?
	kwahntoh ehs lah fyahnthah?
Could I have a receipt for the deposit?	¿Me podría dar un recibo por el pago de la fianza?
	meh pohdreeah dahr oon rehtheeboh pohr ehl pahgoh deh lah fyahnthah?
How much is the surcharge per kilometre?	¿Cuánto hay que pagar extra por kilómetro?
	kwahntoh ay keh pahgahr ehxtrah pohr keelohmehtroh?
Does that include petrol?	¿Está incluida la gasolina?
	ehstah eenklooeedah lah gahsohleenah?
Does that include insurance?	¿Está incluido el seguro?
	ehstah eenklooeedoh ehl sehgooroh?
What time can I pick the...up tomorrow?	¿A qué hora puedo pasar mañana a buscar el/la...?
	ah keh ohrah pwehdoh pahsahr mahnyahnah ah booskahr ehl/lah...?
When does the...have to be back?	¿A qué hora tengo que devolver el/la...?
	ah keh ohrah tehngoh keh dehbohlbehr ehl/lah...?
Where's the petrol tank?	¿Dónde está el depósito de gasolina?
	dohndeh ehstah ehl dehpohseetoh deh gahsohleenah?
What sort of fuel does it take?	¿Qué tipo de combustible hay que echarle?
	keh teepoh deh kohmboosteebleh ay keh ehchahrleh?

5.10 Hitchhiking

Where are you heading?	¿Adónde va?
	ahdohndeh bah?
Can I come along?	¿Me podría llevar?
	meh pohdreeah lyehbahr?
Can my boyfriend/ girlfriend come too?	¿Podría llevar también a mi amigo/amiga?
	pohdreeah lyehbahr tahmbyehn ah mee ahmeegoh/ahmeegah?

On the road

The parts of a bicycle

(the diagram shows the numbered parts)

1 rear lamp	el piloto	*ehl peelohtoh*
2 rear wheel	la rueda trasera	*lah rwehdah trahsehrah*
3 (luggage) carrier	el portaequipajes	*ehl pohrtahehkeepah<u>h</u>ehs*
4 bicycle fork	la cabeza	*lah kahbehthah*
5 bell	el timbre	*ehl teembreh*
inner tube	la cámara	*lah kahmahrah*
tyre	el neumático/la cubierta	*ehl nehoomahteekoh/lah koobyehrtah*
6 crank	la biela	*lah byehlah*
7 gear change	el cambio de velocidades	*ehl kahmbyoh deh behlotheedahdehs*
wire	el hilo	*ehl eeloh*
dynamo	la dinamo	*lah deenahmoh*
bicycle trailer	el remolque de bicicleta	*ehl rehmohlkeh deh beetheeklehtah*
frame	el cuadro	*ehl kwahdroh*
8 dress guard	el guardafaldas	*ehl gwardahfahldahs*
9 chain	la cadena de rodillos	*lah kahdehnah deh rohdeelyohs*
chain guard	el cubrecadena/el cárter	*ehl koobrehkahdehnah/ehl kahrtehr*
chain lock	la cadena antirrobo	*lah kahdehnah ahnteerrohboh*
milometer	el contador kilométrico	*ehl kohntahdohr keelohmehtreekoh*
child's seat	el sillín para niños	*ehl seelyeen pahrah neenyohs*
10 headlamp	el faro	*ehl fahroh*
bulb	la bombilla	*lah bohmbeelyah*
11 pedal	el pedal	*ehl pehdahl*
12 pump	la bombilla	*lah bohmbeelyah*
13 reflector	el cristal reflectante	*ehl kreestahl rehflehktahnteh*
14 brake pad	la zapatilla del freno	*lah thahpahteelyah dehl frehnoh*
15 brake cable	el cable del freno	*ehl kahbleh dehl frehnoh*
16 ring lock	la cerradura	*lah thehrrahdoorah*
17 carrier straps	las bandas elásticas	*lahs bahndahs ehlahsteekahs*
18 spoke	el radio/el rayo	*ehl rahdyoh/ehl rahyoh*
19 mudguard	el guardabarros	*ehl gwahrdahbahrrohs*
20 handlebar	el manillar	*ehl mahneelyahr*
21 chain wheel	el piñón	*ehl peenyohn*
toe clip	el calapiés	*ehl kahlahpyehs*
22 crank axle	el eje del cigueñal	*ehl eh<u>h</u>eh dehl theegwehnyal*
drum brake	el freno de tambor	*ehl frehnoh deh tahmbohr*
23 tube	la llanta	*lah lyahntah*
24 valve	la válvula	*lah bahlboolah*
valve tube	el tubo de la válvula	*ehl tooboh deh lah bahlboolah*

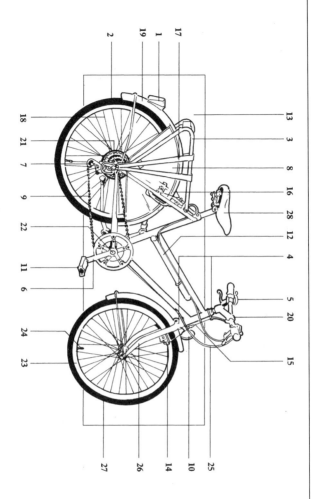

25 gear cable	el cable de velocidades	*ehl kahbleh deh behlohtheedahdehs*
26 fork	la horquilla	*lah ohrkeelyah*
27 front wheel	la rueda delantera	*lah rwehdah dehlahntehrah*
28 seat	el sillín	*el seelyeen*

I'm trying to get to... Voy a...
boy ah...

Is that on the way to...? ¿Eso está camino de...?
ehsoh ehstah kahmeenoh deh...?

Could you drop me off...? ¿Me podría dejar...?
meh pohdreeah dehhahr...?

– here? ¿Me podría dejar aquí mismo?
meh pohdreeah dehhahr ahkee meesmoh?

– at the...exit? ¿Me podría dejar en la salida de...?
meh pohdreeah dehhahr ehn lah sahleedah deh...?

– in the centre? ¿Me podría dejar en el centro?
meh pohdreeah dehhahr ehn ehl thehntroh?

– at the next roundabout? ¿Me podría dejar en la próxima rotonda?
meh pohdreeah dehhahr ehn lah prohxeemah rohtohndah?

Could you stop here, please? ¿Podría pararse aquí?
pohdreeah pahrahrseh ahkee?

I'd like to get out here Quisiera bajarme aquí
keesyehrah bahhahrmeh ahkee

Thanks for the lift Gracias por llevarme
grahthyahs pohr lyehbahrmeh

On the road

5

Public transport

Public transport

6.1 **I**n general

● **The rail network** has been substantially overhauled and expanded and there is now a good, fast service available with the Talgo and Ave in the south. These trains require payment of a supplement and it is advisable to reserve seats in advance, at the station or at travel agencies. Tickets for buses and the metro can be bought at an *estanco*, as well as metro stations.

Announcements

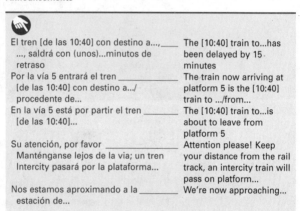

El tren [de las 10:40] con destino a...,___ ..., saldrá con (unos)...minutos de retraso	The [10:40] train to...has been delayed by 15 minutes
Por la vía 5 entrará el tren _____ [de las 10:40] con destino a.../ procedente de...	The train now arriving at platform 5 is the [10:40] train to .../from...
En la vía 5 está por partir el tren _____ [de las 10:40]...	The [10:40] train to...is about to leave from platform 5
Su atención, por favor _____ Manténganse lejos de la via; un tren Intercity pasará por la plataforma...	Attention please! Keep your distance from the rail track, an intercity train will pass on platform...
Nos estamos aproximando a la _____ estación de...	We're now approaching...

Where does this train go to?	¿Adónde va este tren? *ahdohndeh bah ehsteh trehn?*
Does this boat go to...?	¿Este barco va a...? *ehsteh bahrkoh bah ah...?*
Can I take this bus to...?	¿Puedo coger este autobús para ir a...? *pwehdoh kohhehr ehsteh ahootohboos pahrah eer ah...?*
Does this train stop at...?	¿Este tren para en...? *ehsteh trehn pahrah ehn...?*
Is this seat taken/free /reserved?	¿Está ocupado/libre/reservado este asiento? *ehstah ohkoopahdoh/leebreh/rehsehrbahdoh ehsteh ahsyehntoh?*
I've booked...	He reservado... *eh rehsehrbahdoh...*
Could you tell me where I have to get off for... ?	¿Me podría decir dónde me tengo que bajar para ir a...? *meh pohdreeah dehtheer dohndeh meh tehngoh keh bahhar pahrah eer ah...?*
Could you let me know when we get to...?	¿Me podría avisar cuando lleguemos a...? *meh pohdreeah ahbeesahr kwahndoh lyehghehmohs ah...?*
Could you stop at the next stop, please?	La próxima parada, por favor *lah prohxeemah pahrahdah pohr fahbohr*

Where are we now? _____	¿Dónde estamos?
	dohndeh ehstahmohs?
Do I have to get off here? __	¿Tengo que bajarme aquí?
	tehngoh keh bah<u>h</u>ahrmeh ahkee?
Have we already _____ passed...?	¿Ya hemos pasado...?
	yah ehmohs pahsahdoh...?
How long have I been _____ asleep?	¿Cuánto tiempo he dormido?
	kwahntoh tyehmpoh eh dohrmeedoh?
How long does... _____ stop here?	¿Cuánto tiempo se queda aquí...?
	kwahntoh tyehmpoh seh kehdah ahkee?
Can I come back on the ___ same ticket?	¿Este billete me sirve para volver?
	ehsteh beelyehteh meh seerbeh pahrah bohlbehr?
Can I change on this_____ ticket?	¿Se puede hacer trasbordo con este billete?
	seh pwehdeh ahtehehr trahsbohrdoh kohn ehsteh beelyehteh?
How long is this ticket _____ valid for?	¿Hasta cuándo es válido este billete?
	ahstah kwahndoh ehs bahleedoh ehsteh beelyehteh
How much is the _____ supplement for the Talgo/Ave (high speed train)?	¿Cuánto vale el suplemento para el Talgo/el Ave?
	kwahntoh bahleh ehl sooplehmehntoh pahrah ehl tahlgoh/ehl ahbeh?

.2 Questions to passengers

Ticket types

¿Primera o segunda clase? _____	First or second class?
¿Billete de ida o de ida y vuelta? _____	Single or return?
¿Fumadores o no fumadores? _____	Smoking or non-smoking?
¿Ventanilla o pasillo?_____	Window or aisle?
¿Adelante o atrás? _____	Front or back?
¿Asiento o litera? _____	Seat or couchette?
¿Arriba, en el medio o abajo?_____	Top, middle or bottom?
¿Clase turista o preferente?_____	Tourist class or business class?
¿Camarote o butaca? _____	Cabin or seat?
¿Individual o doble? _____	Single or double?
¿Cuántas personas viajan? _____	How many are travelling?

Public transport

Destination

¿Adónde quiere ir? _____	Where are you travelling?
¿Qué día sale? _____	When are you leaving?
Su...sale a las... _____	Your...leaves at...
Tiene que hacer trasbordo _____	You have to change trains
Tiene que bajarse en... _____	You have to get off at...
Tiene que pasar por... _____	You have to travel via...
El viaje de ida es el día... _____	The outward journey is on...
El viaje de vuelta es el día... _____	The return journey is on...
Tiene que embarcar a las...a _____ más tardar	You have to be on board by...

Inside the vehicle

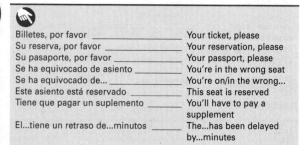

Billetes, por favor _____	Your ticket, please
Su reserva, por favor _____	Your reservation, please
Su pasaporte, por favor _____	Your passport, please
Se ha equivocado de asiento _____	You're in the wrong seat
Se ha equivocado de... _____	You're on/in the wrong...
Este asiento está reservado _____	This seat is reserved
Tiene que pagar un suplemento _____	You'll have to pay a supplement
El...tiene un retraso de...minutos _____	The...has been delayed by...minutes

6 .3 Tickets

Where can I...? _____	¿Dónde...? *dohndeh...?*
– buy a ticket? _____	¿Dónde se compran los billetes? *dohndeh seh kohmprahn lohs beelyehtehs?*
– make a reservation? _____	¿Dónde se hacen las reservas? *dohndeh seh ahthehn lahs rehsehrbahs?*
– book a flight? _____	¿Dónde puedo hacer una reserva para un vuelo? *dohndeh pwehdoh ahtehr oonah rehsehrbah pahrah oon bwehloh?*
Could I have a...to..., please? _____	Quiero un/una...a... *kyehroh oon/oonah...ah...*
– a single _____	Quiero un billete de ida a... *kyehroh oon beelyehteh deh eedah ah...*
– a return _____	Quiero un billete de ida y vuelta a... *kyehroh oon beelyehteh deh eedah ee bwehltah ah...*
first class _____	en primera clase *ehn preemehrah klahseh*
second class _____	en segunda clase *ehn sehgoondah klahseh*

60

tourist class _____	en clase turista
	ehn klahseh tooreestah
business class _____	en clase preferente
	ehn klahseh prehfehrehnteh
I'd like to book a _____ seat/couchette/cabin	Quisiera reservar un asiento/una litera/un camarote
	keesyehrah rehsehrbah oon ahsyehntoh/oonah leetehrah/oon kahmahrohteh
I'd like to book a berth _____ in the sleeping car	Quisiera reservar una plaza en un coche cama
	keesyehrah rehsehrbah oonah plahthah ehn oon kohcheh kahmah
top/middle/bottom _____	arriba/en el medio/abajo
	ahrreebah/ehn ehl mehdyoh/ahbahhoh
smoking/no smoking _____	fumadores/no fumadores
	foomahdohrehs/noh foomahdohrehs
by the window _____	ventanilla
	behntahneelyah
single/double _____	individual/doble
	eendeebeedwahl/dohbleh
at the front/back _____	adelante/atrás
	ahdehlahnteh/ahtrahs
There are...of us _____	Somos...personas
	sohmohs...pehrsohnahs
a car _____	un coche
	oon kohcheh
a caravan _____	una caravana
	oonah kahrahbahnah
...bicycles _____	...bicicletas
	...beetheeklehtahs
Do you also have...? _____	¿Tienen...?
	tyehnehn...?
– season tickets? _____	¿Tienen billetes para varios viajes?
	tyehnen beelyehtehs pahrah bahryohs byahhehs?
– weekly tickets? _____	¿Tienen abonos semanales?
	tyehnehn ahbohnohs sehmahnahlehs?
– monthly season tickets? _____	¿Tienen abonos mensuales?
	tyehnehn ahbohnohs mehnswahlehs?

6 .4 Information

Where's-? _____	¿Dónde hay...?
	dohndeh ay...?
Where's the information _____ desk?	¿Dónde está la oficina de información?
	dohndeh ehstah lah ohfeetheenah deh eenfohrmahthyohn?
Where can I find a _____ timetable?	¿Dónde hay un horario?
	dohndeh ay oon ohrahryoh?
Where's the...desk? _____	¿Dónde está el mostrador de...?
	dohndeh ehstah ehl mohstrahdohr deh...?
Do you have a city map _____ with the bus/the underground routes on it?	¿Tendría un plano de la ciudad con la red de autobuses/metro?
	tehndreeah oon plahnoh deh lah thyoodahdh kohn lah rehth deh ahootohboosehs/mehtroh?

Do you have a _____ timetable?	¿Tendría un horario? *tehndreeah oon ohrahryoh?*
I'd like to confirm/_____ cancel/change my booking for/trip to...	Quisiera confirmar/cancelar/cambiar mi reserva/mi viaje a... *keesyehrah kohnfeermahr/kahnthehlahr/kahmbyahr mee rehsehrbah/mee byahheh ah...*
Will I get my money _____ back?	¿Me devuelven el dinero? *meh dehbwehlbehn ehl deenehroh?*
I want to go to... _____ How do I get there? (What's the quickest way there?)	Tengo que ir a...¿Cómo hago para llegar (lo más rápido posible)? *tehngoh keh eer ah...kohmoh ahgoh pahrah lyehgahr(loh mahs rahpeedoh pohseebleh)?*
How much is a _____ single/return to...?	¿Cuánto vale un billete de ida/de ida y vuelta a...? *kwahntoh bahleh oon beelyehteh deh eedah ee bwehltah ah...?*
Do I have to pay a_____ supplement?	¿Tengo que pagar algún suplemento? *tehngoh keh pahgahr ahlgoon sooplehmehntoh?*
Can I interrupt my_____ journey with this ticket?	¿Con este billete puedo hacer una parada intermedia? *kohn ehsteh beelyehteh pwehdoh ahthehr oonah pahrahdah eentehrmehdyah?*
How much luggage _____ am I allowed?	¿Cuánto equipaje puedo llevar? *kwahntoh ehkeepahheh pwehdoh lyebahr?*
Can I send my luggage _____ in advance?	¿Puedo enviar mi equipaje por anticipado? *pwehdoh ehnbeeahr mee ehkeepahheh pohr ahnteetheepahdoh?*
Does this...travel direct? _____	¿Este...va directo? *ehsteh...bah deerehktoh?*
Do I have to change? _____ Where?	¿Tengo que hacer trasbordo? ¿Dónde? *tehngoh keh ahthehr trahsbohrdoh? dohndeh?*
Will there be any _____ stopovers?	¿Habrá escalas? *ahbrah ehskahlahs?*
Does the boat call in at _____ any ports on the way?	¿El barco hace alguna escala? *ehl bahrkoh ahtheh ahlgoonah ehskahlah?*
Does the train/ _____ bus stop at...?	¿Este tren/este autobús para en...? *ehsteh trehn/ehsteh ahootohboos pahrah ehn...?*
Where should I get off? _____	¿Dónde me tengo que bajar? *dohndeh meh tehngoh keh bahhahr?*
Is there a connection _____ to...?	¿Hay enlace para...? *ay ehnlahtheh pahrah...?*
How long do I have to _____ wait?	¿Cuánto tengo que esperar? *kwahntoh tehngoh keh ehspehrahr?*
When does...leave?_____	¿Cuándo sale...? *kwahndoh sahleh...?*
What time does the _____ first/next/last...leave?	¿A qué hora sale el primer/próximo/último...? *ah keh ohrah sahleh ehl preemehr/prohxeemoh/oolteemoh...?*
How long does...take? _____	¿Cuánto tarda...en llegar? *kwahntoh tahrdah...ehn lyehgahr?*

Could you get me _____	¿Podría llamar un taxi?
a taxi, please?	*pohdreeah lyahmahr oon tahxee?*
Is there any mail _____	¿Hay carta para mí?
for me?	*ay kahrtah pahrah mee?*

.2 Camping

See the diagram on page 69.

Puede elegir el sitio usted mismo _____	You can pick your own site
El sitio se lo asignamos nosotros _____	You'll be allocated a site
Este es el número de su _____ emplazamiento	This is your site number
Por favor pegue esto en el parabrisas ___ del coche	Stick this on your car, please
No pierda esta tarjeta _____	Please don't lose this card

Where's the manager? _____	¿Dónde está el encargado?
	dohnde ehstah ehl ehnkahrgahdoh?
Are we allowed to _____ camp here?	¿Podemos acampar aquí?
	pohdehmohs ahkahmpahr ahkee?
There are...of us and _____ ...tents	Somos...personas y...tiendas
	sohmohs...pehrsohnahs ee...tyehndahs
Can we pick our _____ own site?	¿Podemos elegir el sitio nosotros mismos?
	pohdehmohs ehlehheer ehl seetyoh nohsohtrohs meesmohs?
Do you have a quiet _____ spot for us?	¿Nos podría dar un sitio tranquilo?
	nohs pohdreeah dahr oon seetyoh trahnkeeloh?
Do you have any other ___ sites available?	¿No tiene otro sitio libre?
	noh tyehneh ohtroh seetyoh leebreh?
It's too windy/sunny/ _____ shady here.	Hay mucho viento/mucho sol/mucha sombra
	ay moochoh byehntoh/moochoh sohl/moochah sohmbrah
It's too crowded here _____	Hay mucha gente
	ay moochah hehnteh
The ground's too _____ hard/uneven	El suelo es muy duro/muy desigual
	ehl swehloh ehs mwee dooroh/mwee dehseegwahl
Do you have a level _____ spot for the camper/caravan/folding caravan?	¿Tiene un sitio plano para el autocaravana/la caravana/el remolque tienda?
	tyehneh oon seetyoh plahnoh pahrah ehl ahootohkahrahbahnah/lah kahrahbahnah/ehl rehmohlkeh-tyehndah?
Could we have _____ adjoining sites?	¿Tiene dos plazas juntas?
	tyehneh dohs plahthahs hoontahs?
Can we park the car _____ next to the tent?	¿Podemos aparcar el coche junto a la tienda?
	pohdehmohs ahpahrkahr ehl kohcheh hoontoh ah lah tyehndah?

Overnight accommodation

Camping equipment
(the diagram shows the numbered parts)

luggage space	el compartimiento de equipaje	*ehl kohmpahrteemyehntoh de ehkeepahhheh*
can opener	el abrelatas	*ehl ahbrehlahtahs*
butane gas bottle	la bombona (de gas butano)	*lah bohmbohnah (deh gahs bootahnoh)*
1 pannier	la ciclobolsa	*lah theeklohbohlsah*
2 gas cooker	el hornillo de gas	*ehl ohrneelyoh deh gahs*
3 groundsheet	la lona del suelo	*lah lohnah dehl swehloh*
mallet	el martillo	*ehl mahrteelyoh*
hammock	la hamaca	*lah ahmahkah*
4 jerry can	el bidón	*ehl beedohn*
campfire	la fogata	*lah fohgahtah*
5 folding chair	la silla plegable	*lah seelyah plehgahbleh*
6 insulated picnic box	la nevera portátil/la bolsa nevera	*lah nehbehrah pohrtahteel/lah bohlsah nehbehrah*
ice pack	el acumulador	*ehl akoomoolahdohr*
compass	la brújula	*lah broohoolah*
wick	la mecha	*lah mehchah*
corkscrew	el sacacorchos	*ehl sahkahkohrchohs*
7 airbed	el colchón neumático	*ehl kohlchohn nehoomahteekoh*
8 airbed plug	el taponcito de la válvula del colchón	*ehl tahpohntheetoh deh lah bahlboolah dehl kohlchohn*
pump	la bomba neumática	*lah bohmbah nehoomahteekah*
9 awning	el tejadillo	*ehl tehhahdeelyoh*
10 karimat	la esterilla	*lah ehstehreelyah*
11 pan	la olla	*lah ohlyah*
12 pan handle	el mango de la olla	*ehl mahngoh deh lah ohlyah*
primus stove	el hornillo de querosén	*ehl ohrneelyoh deh kehrohsehn*
zip	la cremallera	*lah krehmalyehrah*
13 backpack	la mochila	*lah mohcheelah*
14 guy rope	el viento	*ehl byehntoh*
sleeping bag	el saco de dormir	*ehl sahkoh deh dohrmeer*
15 storm lantern	el farol de tormentas	*ehl fahrohl deh tohrmehntahs*
camp bed	el catre (de tijera)	*ehl kahtreh (deh teehehrah)*
table	la mesa	*lah mehsah*
16 tent	la tienda	*lah tyehndah*
17 tent peg	la estaca	*lah ehstakah*
18 tent pole	el palo de tienda	*ehl pahloh deh tyehndah*
vacuum flask	el termo	*ehl tehrmoh*
19 water bottle	la cantimplora	*lah kahnteemplohrah*
clothes peg	la pinza	*lah peenthah*
clothes line	la cuerda de tender ropa	*lah kwehrdah deh tehndehr rohpah*
windbreak	el paravientos/el paraván	*ehl pahrahbyehntohs/ehl pahrahbahn*
20 torch	la linterna de bolsillo	*lah leentehrnah deh bohlseelyoh*
pocket knife	la navaja	*lah nahbahhhah*

Overnight accommodation

7

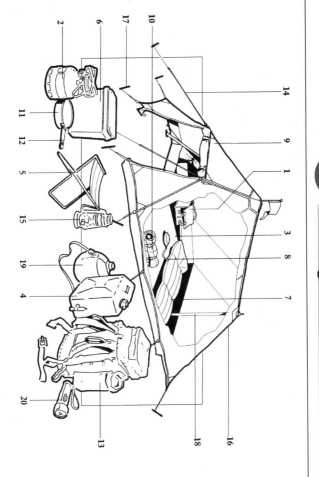

How much is it per person/tent/caravan/car?	¿Cuánto sale por persona/tienda/caravana/coche?
	kwahntoh sahleh pohr pehrsohnah/tyehndah/kahrahbahnah/kohcheh?
Are there any...?	¿Hay...?
	ay...?
– any hot showers?	¿Hay duchas con agua caliente?
	ay doochahs kohn ahgwah kahlyehnteh?
– washing machines?	¿Hay lavadoras?
	ay lahbahdohrahs?
Is there a...on the site?	¿En este camping hay...?
	ehn ehsteh kahmpeen ay...?
Is there a children's play area on the site?	¿En este camping hay un sitio para que jueguen los niños?
	ehn ehsteh kahmpeen ay oon seetyoh pahrah keh hwehghehn lohs neenyohs?
Are there covered cooking facilities on the site?	¿En este camping hay un sitio cubierto para cocinar?
	ehn ehsteh kahmpeen ay oon seetyoh koobyehrtoh pahrah kohtheenahr?
Can I rent a safe here?	¿Tienen caja fuerte para alquilar?
	tyehnehn kahhah fwehrteh pahrah ahlkeelahr?
Are we allowed to barbecue here?	¿Se pueden hacer barbacoas?
	seh pwehdehn ahtehr bahrbahkohahs?
Are there any power points?	¿Hay tomas de corriente eléctrica?
	ay tohmahs deh kohrryehnteh ehlehktreekah?
Is there drinking water?	¿Hay agua potable?
	ay ahgwah pohtahbleh?
When's the rubbish collected?	¿Cuándo pasan a recoger la basura?
	kwahndoh pahsahn ah rehkohhehr lah bahsoorah?
Do you sell gas bottles (butane gas/propane gas)?	¿Venden bombonas de gas (butano/propano)?
	behndehn bohmbohnahs deh gahs(bootahnoh/prohpahnoh)?

7.3 Hotel/B&B/apartment/holiday house

Do you have a single/double room available?	¿Le queda alguna habitación individual/doble?
	leh kehdah ahlgoonah ahbeetahthyohn eendeebeedwahl/dohbleh?
per person/per room	por persona/por habitación
	pohr pehrsohnah/pohr ahbeetahthyohn
Does that include breakfast/lunch/dinner?	¿Incluye desayuno/comida/cena?
	eenklooyeh dehsahyoonoh/kohmeedah/thehnah?
Could we have two adjoining rooms?	¿Nos puede dar dos habitaciones una al lado de la otra?
	nohs pwehdeh dahr dohs ahbeetahthyohnehs oonah ahl lahdoh deh lah ohtrah?
with/without toilet/bath/shower	con/sin lavabo propio/baño propio/ducha propia
	kohn/seen lahbahboh prohpyoh/bahnyoh prohpyo/doochah prohpyah?

70

(not) facing the street	que (no) dé a la calle
	keh (noh) deh ah lah kahlyeh
with/without a view of the sea	con/sin vista al mar
	kohn/seen beestah ahl mahr
Is there...in the hotel?	¿El hotel tiene...?
	ehl ohtehl tyehneh...?
Is there a lift in the hotel?	¿El hotel tiene ascensor?
	ehl ohtehl tyehneh ahsthehnsohr?
Do you have room service?	¿El hotel tiene servicio de habitación?
	ehl ohtehl tyehneh sehrbeethyoh deh ahbeetahthyohn?

Tiene lavabo y ducha en el mismo piso/en su habitación	You can find the toilet and shower on the same floor/en suite
Por aquí, por favor	This way, please
Su habitación está en el...piso; es la número...	Your room is on the...floor, number...

Could I see the room?	¿Puedo ver la habitación?
	pwehdoh behr lah ahbeetahthyohn?
I'll take this room	Me quedo con esta habitación
	meh kehdoh kohn ehstah abeetathyohn
We don't like this one	Esta no nos gusta
	ehstah noh nohs goostah
Do you have a larger/less expensive room?	¿Tiene una habitación más grande/más barata?
	tyehneh oonah ahbeetathyohn mahs grahnde/mahs bahrahtah?
Could you put in a cot?	¿Puede agregar una cuna?
	pwehde ahgrehgahr oonah koonah?
What time's breakfast?	¿A qué hora es el desayuno?
	ah keh ohrah ehs ehl dehsahyoonoh?
Where's the dining room?	¿Dónde está el comedor?
	dohndeh ehstah ehl kohmehdohr?
Can I have breakfast in my room?	¿Me pueden traer el desayuno a la habitación?
	meh pwehdehn trahehr ehl dehsahyoonoh ah lah ahbeetahthyohn?
Where's the emergency exit/fire escape?	¿Dónde está la salida de emergencia/la escalera de incendios?
	dohndeh ehstah lah sahleedah deh ehmehrhehnthyah/lah ehskahlehrah de eentehndyohs?
Where can I park my car (safely)?	¿Dónde hay un sitio (seguro) para aparcar el coche?
	dohndeh ay oon seetyoh sehgooroh pahrah ahpahrkahr ehl kohcheh?
The key to room..., please	La llave de la habitación..., por favor
	lah lyahbeh deh lah ahbeetahthyohn..., pohr fahbohr
Could you put this in the safe, please?	¿Podría dejar esto en la caja fuerte?
	pohdreeah dehhahr ehstoh ehn lah cahhah fwehrteh?

71

Could you wake me _____ at...tomorrow?	¿Me podría despertar mañana a las...?
	meh pohdreeah dehspehrtahr mahnyahnah ah lahs...?
Could you find a _____ babysitter for me?	¿Me podría conseguir una niñera para el bebé?
	meh pohdreeah kohnsehgeer oonah neenyehrah pahrah ehl behbeh?
Could I have an extra_____ blanket?	¿Tendría una manta extra?
	tehndreeah oonah mahntah ehxtrah?
What days do the _____ cleaners come in?	¿Qué días limpian la habitación?
	keh deeahs leempyahn lah ahbeetahthyohn?
When are the sheets/ _____ towels/tea towels changed?	¿Cuándo cambian las sábanas/las toallas/los paños de cocina?
	kwahndoh kahmbyahn lahs sahbahnahs/lahs tohahlyahs/lohs pahnyohs deh kohtheenah?

7.4 Complaints

We can't sleep for _____ the noise	No podemos dormir por el ruido
	noh pohdehmohs dohrmeer pohr ehl rweedoh
Could you turn the _____ radio down, please?	¿Podría bajar el volumen de la radio?
	pohdreeah bahhahr ehl vohloomehn deh lah rahdyoh?
We're out of toilet paper ___	Se ha acabado el papel higiénico.
	seh ah ahkahbahdoh ehl pahpehl eehyehneekoh
There aren't any.../ _____ there's not enough...	No hay.../no hay suficientes...
	noh ay.../noh ay soofeethyehntehs...
The bed linen's dirty_____	La ropa de cama está sucia
	lah rohpah deh kahmah ehstah soothyah
The room hasn't been _____ cleaned.	No han limpiado la habitación
	noh ahn leempyahdoh lah ahbeetahthyohn
The kitchen is not clean___	La cocina no está limpia
	lah kohtheenah noh ehstah leempyah
The kitchen utensils are___ dirty	Los utensilios de cocina están sucios
	lohs ootehnseelyohs deh kohtheenah ehstahn soothyohs
The heater's not_____ working	La calefacción no funciona
	lah kahlehfahkthyohn noh foonthyohnah
There's no (hot) _____ water/electricity	No hay agua (caliente)/electricidad
	noh ay ahgwah(kahlyehnteh)/ehlehktreetheedahdh
...is broken_____	...está estropeado
	...ehstah ehstrohpehahdoh
Could you have that _____ seen to?	¿Podrían hacerlo ver?
	pohdreeahn ahthehrloh behr?
Could I have another _____ room/site?	¿Tendría otra habitación/sitio para la tienda?
	tehndreeah ohtrah abeetahthyohn/seetyoh pahrah lah tyehndah?
The bed creaks terribly ___	La cama hace mucho ruido
	lah kahmah ahtheh moochoh rweedoh
The bed sags _____	La cama es demasiado blanda
	lah kahmah ehs dehmahsyahdoh blahndah

There are bugs/insects in our room	Hay muchos bichos/insectos en nuestra habitación
	ay moochohs beechohs/eensehktohs ehn nwehstrah ahbeetahthyohn
This place is full of mosquitos	Está lleno de mosquitos
	ehstah lyehnoh deh mohskeetohs
– cockroaches	Está lleno de cucarachas
	ehstah lyehnoh deh kookahrahchahs
– Brits	Está lleno de ingleses
	ehstah lyehnoh deh eenglehsehs

🕖 .5 Departure

See also 8.2 Settling the bill

I'm leaving tomorrow. Could I settle my bill, please?	Mañana me voy. ¿Podría pagar la cuenta ahora?
	mahnyahnah meh boy. pohdreeah pahgahr lah kwehntah ahohrah?
What time should we vacate?	¿A qué hora tenemos que dejar...?
	ah keh ohrah tehnehmohs keh dehhahr...?
Could I have my deposit/passport back, please?	¿Me devuelve la fianza/el pasaporte?
	meh dehbwehlbeh lah fyahnthah/ehl pahsahpohrteh?
We're in a terrible hurry	Llevamos mucha prisa
	lyehbahmohs moochah preesah
Could you forward my mail to this address?	¿Podría enviarme la correspondencia a esta dirección?
	pohdreeah ehnbyahrmeh lah kohrrehspohndehnthyah ah ehstah deerehkthyohn?
Could we leave our luggage here until we leave?	¿Podríamos dejar las maletas aquí hasta que nos marchemos?
	pohdreeahmohs dehhahr lahs mahlehtahs ahkee ahstah keh nohs mahrchehmohs?
Thanks for your hospitality	Muchas gracias por la hospitalidad
	moochahs grahthyahs pohr lah ohspeetahleedahdh

Money matters

Money matters **8**

● **In general,** banks are open to the public between 9am and 2pm; they are closed on Saturdays. In large cities it is possible to find main branches open until 4.30. To exchange currency a passport is required. Some travel agencies also provide facilities. The sign *cambio* indicates that money can be exchanged. Hotels may also offer this service, but at a less favourable rate.

8 .1 **B**anks

Where can I find a_____ bank/an exchange office around here?	¿Dónde hay un banco/una oficina de cambios por aquí? *dohndeh ay oon bahnkoh/oonah ohfeetheenah deh kahmbyohs pohr ahkee?*
Where can I cash this_____ traveller's cheque/giro cheque?	¿Dónde puedo cambiar este cheque de viajero/este cheque postal? *dohndeh pwehdoh kahmbyahr ehsteh chehkeh deh byah<u>h</u>ehroh/eh<u>s</u>teh chehkeh pohstahl?*
Can I cash this...here? _____	¿Puedo cambiar aquí este...? *pwehdoh kahmbyahr ahkee ehsteh...?*
Can I withdraw money_____ on my credit card here?	¿Se puede sacar dinero con una tarjeta de crédito? *seh pwehdeh sahkahr deenehroh kohn oonah tahr<u>h</u>ehtah deh krehdeetoh?*
What's the minimum/_____ maximum amount?	¿Cuál es el mínimo/el máximo? *kwahl ehs ehl meeneemoh/ehl mahxeemoh?*
Can I take out less_____ than that?	¿También puedo sacar menos? *tahmbyehn pwehdoh sahkahr mehnohs?*
I've had some money_____ transferred here. Has it arrived yet?	He pedido un giro telegráfico. ¿Me ha llegado ya? *eh pehdeedoh oon <u>h</u>eeroh tehlehgrahfeekoh. meh ah lyehgahdoh yah?*
These are the details _____ of my bank in the UK	Estos son los datos de mi banco en el Reino Unido *ehstohs sohn lohs dahtohs deh mee bahnkoh ehn ehl reynoh ooneedoh*
This is my bank/giro_____ number	Este es mi número de cuenta bancaria/de la caja postal *ehsteh ehs mee noomehroh deh kwehntah bahnkahryah/deh lah kah<u>h</u>ah pohstahl*
I'd like to change _____ some money	Quisiera cambiar dinero *keesyehrah kahmbyahr deenehroh*
– pounds into... _____	Libras esterlinas por... *leebrahs ehstehrleenahs pohr...*
– dollars into... _____	Dólares estadounidenses por... *dohlahrehs ehstahdohooneedehnsehs pohr...*
What's the exchange _____ rate?	¿A cuánto está el cambio? *ah kwahntoh ehstah ehl kahmbyoh?*
Could you give me _____ some small change with it?	¿Me podría dar sencillo/cambio? *meh pohdreeah dahr sehntheelyoh/kahmbyoh?*
This is not right _____	Esto está mal *ehstoh ehstah mahl*

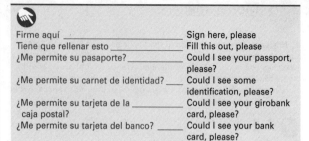

8.2 Settling the bill

Could you put it on my bill?
¿Podría cargarlo a mi cuenta?
pohdreeah kahrgahrloh ah mee kwehntah?

Does this amount include service?
¿Está incluido el servicio en esta cifra?
ehstah eenklooeedoh ehl sehrbeethyoh ehn ehstah theefrah?

Can I pay by...?
¿Puedo pagar con...?
pwehdoh pahgahr kohn...?

Can I pay by credit card?
¿Puedo pagar con tarjeta de crédito?
pwehdoh pahgahr kohn tahrhehtah deh krehdeetoh?

Can I pay by traveller's cheque?
¿Puedo pagar con un cheque de viajero?
pwehdoh pahgahr kohn oon chehkeh de byahhehroh?

Can I pay with foreign currency?
¿Puedo pagar con moneda extranjera?
pwehdoh pahgahr kohn mohnehdah ehxtrahnhehrah?

You've given me too much/you haven't given me enough change
Me ha devuelto de más/de menos
meh ah dehbwehltoh deh mahs/deh mehnohs

Could you check the bill again, please?
¿Puede volver a hacer la cuenta?
pwehdeh bohlbehr ah ahthehr lah kwehntah?

Could I have a receipt, please?
¿Podría darme un recibo?
pohdreeah dahrmeh oon rehtheeboh?

I don't have enough money on me
No me alcanza el dinero
noh meh ahlkahnthah ehl deenehroh

This is for you
Tenga, esto es para usted
tehngah, ehstoh ehs pahrah oostehdh

Keep the change
Quédese con la vuelta
kehdehseh kohn lah bwehltah

Post and telephone

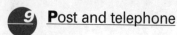

9 Post and telephone

9.1 Post

For giros, see 8 Money matters

● **Post offices** are open from Monday to Saturday from 9am to 1 or 1.30pm. However stamps (*sellos*) can be bought at any *estanco* and many hotels also provide stamps. It is advisable to post letters at a post office, rather than the yellow mail boxes (*buzón*).

giros postales	telegramas	sellos
money orders	telegrams	stamps
paquetes		
parcels		

Where's...?	¿Dónde está...?
	dohndeh ehstah...?
Where's the post office?	¿Dónde hay una oficina de Correos por aquí?
	dohndeh ay oonah ohfeetheenah deh kohrrehohs pohr ahkee?
Where's the main post office?	¿Dónde está la oficina central de Correos?
	dohndeh ehstah lah ohfeetheenah thehntrahl deh kohrrehohs?
Where's the postbox?	¿Dónde hay un buzón por aquí?
	dohndeh ahee oon boothohn pohr ahkee?
Which counter should I go to...?	¿Cuál es la ventanilla para...?
	kwahl ehs lah behntahneelyah pahrah...?
– to send a fax	¿Cuál es la ventanilla para enviar un fax?
	kwahl ehs lah behntahneelyah pahrah ehnbyahr oon fahx?
– to change money	¿Cuál es la ventanilla para cambiar dinero?
	kwahl ehs lah behntahneelyah pahrah kahmbyahr deenehroh?
– to change giro cheques	¿Cuál es la ventanilla para los cheques postales?
	kwahl ehs lah behntahneelyah pahrah lohs chehkehs pohstahlehs?
– for a Telegraph Money Order?	¿Cuál es la ventanilla para los giros telegráficos?
	kwahl ehs lah behntahneelyah pahrah lohs heerohs tehlehgrahfeekohs?
Poste restante	Lista de correos
	leestah deh kohrrehohs
Is there any mail for me? My name's...	¿Hay carta para mí? Me llamo...
	ay kahrtah pahrah mee? meh lyahmoh...

Stamps

What's the postage _____ for a...to...?	¿Cuánto se le pone a un(a)...para...?
	kwahntoh seh leh pohneh ah oon(ah)...pahrah...?
Are there enough _____ stamps on it?	¿Lleva suficiente franqueo?
	lyehbah soofeethyehnteh frahnkehoh?
I'd like... ...peseta stamps __	Déme...sellos de...
	dehmeh...sehlyohs deh...
I'd like to send this... _____	Quisiera enviar esto...
	keesyehrah ehnbyahr ehstoh...
– express _____	Quisiera enviar esto por correo urgente
	keesyehrah ehnbyahr ehstoh pohr kohrrehoh oorhehnteh
– by air mail _____	Quisiera enviar esto por avión
	keesyehrah ehnbyahr ehstoh pohr ahbyohn
– by registered mail _____	Quisiera enviar esto certificado
	keesyehrah ehnbyahr ehstoh thehrteefeekahdoh

Telegram / fax

I'd like to send a _____ telegram to...	Quisiera mandar un telegrama a...
	keesyehrah mahndahr oon tehlehgrahmah ah...
How much is that _____ per word?	¿Cuánto cuesta por palabra?
	kwahntoh kwehstah pohr pahlahbrah?
This is the text I want _____ to send	Este es el texto que quiero enviar
	ehsteh ehs ehl tehxtoh keh kyehroh ehnbyahr
Shall I fill in the form _____ myself?	¿Relleno yo mismo el formulario?
	rehlyehnoh yoh meesmoh ehl fohrmoolahryoh?
Can I make photocopies/__ send a fax here?	¿Se pueden hacer fotocopias/se puede enviar un fax aquí?
	seh pwehdehn ahtehr fohtohkohpyahs/seh pwehdeh ehnbyahr oon fahx ahkee?
How much is it _____ per page?	¿Cuánto cuesta por página?
	kwahntoh kwehstah pohr pah<u>h</u>eenah?

.2 Telephone

See also 1.8 Telephone alphabet

● **All phone booths** offer a direct international service to the UK or US (07 - country code 44 (UK) or 1 (US) – trunk code minus 0 – number). Area codes are displayed. It is easier, and may even be cheaper to place your call from the *Telefónica* or telephone office. When phoning someone in Spain, you will not be greeted with the subscriber's name but *diga* or *dígame*.

Is there a phone box _____ around here?	¿Hay alguna cabina telefónica por aquí?
	ay ahlgoonah kahbeenah tehlehfohneekah pohr ahkee?
Could I use your _____ phone, please?	¿Podría usar su teléfono?
	pohdreeah oosahr soo tehlehfohnoh?

Do you have a _____ ¿Tiene una guía de teléfonos de la
(city/region)...phone ciudad/la provincia de...?
directory? *tyehneh oonah gheeah deh tehlehfohnohs*
deh lah thyoodahdh/lah prohbeenthyah
deh...?

Where can I get a _____ ¿Dónde puedo conseguir una tarjeta de
phone card? teléfonos?
dohndeh pwehdoh kohnsehgheer oonah
tarrhehtah deh tehlehfohnohs?

Could you give me...? _____ ¿Me podría dar...?
meh pohdreeah dahr...?

– the number for _____ ¿Me podría dar el número de información
international directory internacional?
enquiries *meh pohdreeah dahr ehl noomehroh deh*
eenfohrmahthyohn eentehrnahthyohnahl?

– the number of room... ___ ¿Me podría dar el número de la
habitación...?
meh pohdreeah dahr ehl noomehroh deh lah
ahbeetahthyohn...?

– the international _____ ¿Me podría dar el indicativo
access code internacional?
meh pohdreeah dahr ehl eendeekahteeboh
eentehrnahthyonahl...?

– the country code for..._____ ¿Me podría dar el indicativo de...?
meh pohdreeah dahr ehl eendeekahteeboh
deh...?

– the trunk code for... _____ ¿Me podría dar el prefijo de...?
meh pohdreeah dahr ehl prehfeehoh deh...?

– the number of... _____ ¿Me podría dar el número de abonado
de...?
meh pohdreeah dahr ehl noomehroh deh
ahbohnahdoh deh...?

Could you check if this _____ ¿Podría controlar si está bien este
number's correct? número?
pohdreeah kohntrohlahr see ehstah byehn
ehsteh noomehroh?

Can I dial international_____ ¿Se puede llamar directamente al
direct? extranjero?
seh pwehdeh lyahmahr deerehktahmehnteh
ahl ehxtrahnhehroh?

Do I have to go through ___ ¿Hay que llamar por operadora?
the switchboard? *ay keh lyahmahr pohr ohpehrahdohrah?*

Do I have to dial '0'_____ ¿Hay que marcar primero el cero?
first? *ay keh mahrkahr preemehroh ehl thehroh?*

Do I have to book _____ ¿Hay que pedir línea?
my calls? *ay keh pehdeer leenehah?*

Could you dial this _____ ¿Podría usted llamar a este número?
number for me, please? *pohdreeah oostehdh lyahmahr ah ehsteh*
noomehroh?

Could you put me _____ ¿Me podría poner con.../con la
through to.../extension..., extensión...?
please? *meh pohdreeah pohnehr kohn.../kohn lah*
ehxtehnsyohn...?

I'd like to place a _____ Quisiera una llamada de cobro revertido
reverse-charge call to... a...
keesyehrah oonah lyahmahdah deh kohbroh
rehbehrteedoh ah...

What's the charge per minute?	¿Cuánto cuesta por minuto?
	kwahntoh kwehstah pohr meenootoh?
Have there been any calls for me?	¿Ha habido alguna llamada para mí?
	ah ahbeedoh ahlgoonah lyahmahdah pahrah mee?

The conversation

Hello, this is... _____	Buenos días, soy...
	bwehnohs deeahs, soy...
Who is this, please? _____	¿Con quién hablo?
	kohn kyehn ahbloh?
Is this...? _____	¿Hablo con...?
	ahbloh kohn...?
I'm sorry, I've dialled the wrong number	Perdone, me he equivocado de número
	pehrdohneh, meh eh ehkeebohkahdoh deh noomehroh
I can't hear you _____	No le oigo bien
	noh leh oygoh byehn
I'd like to speak to... _____	Quisiera hablar con...
	keesyehrah ahblahr kohn...
Is there anybody who speaks English?	¿Hay alguien que hable inglés?
	ay ahlghyehn keh ahbleh eenglehs?
Extension..., please _____	¿Me pone con la extensión...?
	meh pohneh kohn lah ehxtehnsyohn...?
Could you ask him/her to call me back?	¿Podría decirle que me llame?
	pohdreeah dehteerleh keh meh lyahmeh?
My name's... _____ My number's...	Me llamo...Mi número es...
	meh lyahmoh...mee noomehroh ehs...
Could you tell him/her I called?	¿Puede decirle que he llamado?
	pwehdeh dehteerleh keh eh lyahmahdoh?
I'll call back tomorrow _____	Lo/la volveré a llamar mañana
	loh/lah bohlbehreh ah lyahmahr mahnyahnah

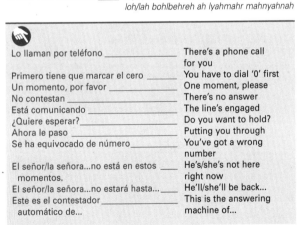

Lo llaman por teléfono _____	There's a phone call for you
Primero tiene que marcar el cero _____	You have to dial '0' first
Un momento, por favor _____	One moment, please
No contestan _____	There's no answer
Está comunicando _____	The line's engaged
¿Quiere esperar? _____	Do you want to hold?
Ahora le paso _____	Putting you through
Se ha equivocado de número _____	You've got a wrong number
El señor/la señora...no está en estos momentos.	He's/she's not here right now
El señor/la señora...no estará hasta... ___	He'll/she'll be back...
Este es el contestador automático de...	This is the answering machine of...

Shopping

10

⑩ **S**hopping

● **Opening times:** Monday to Friday, 9.30am-1.30pm and 5pm-8pm.
Department stores are open in the afternoons from 4pm and remain
open on Saturdays. Other shops generally close on Saturdays at 1pm.
In tourist areas shops open for longer periods.
Chemists display the list of *farmacias de guardia* (those open on
Sundays and after hours).

almacén department store	droguería household products and cosmetics	panadería bakery
antigüedades antiques	electrodomésticos electrical appliances	pastelería cake shop
artículos de deporte sports shop	estanco tobacconist	peluquería (señoras, caballeros) hairdresser
artículos del hogar household goods	farmacia chemist	perfumería cosmetics
artículos dietéticos health food shop	ferretería hardware shop	pescadería fishmonger
artículos fotográficos camera shop	floristería florist	quiosco news stand
artículos usados second hand goods	frutas y verduras greengrocer	recuerdos de viaje souvenir shop
autoservicio self service	galería comercial shopping arcade	reparación de bicicletas bicycle repair shop
bicicletas bicycle shop	heladería ice cream parlour	revistas y prensa newsagent
bodega off licence	joyería jeweller	salón de belleza beauty parlour
bricolaje DIY-store	juguetería toy shop	supermercado supermarket
carnicería butcher's shop	lavandería laundry	tienda shop
casa de música music shop	lechería dairy	tienda de modas clothes shop
centro comercial shopping centre	librería book shop	tintorería drycleaner
comestibles grocery store	mercado market	zapatería shoe shop
decoración (de interiores) interior design shop	mercería draper óptica optician	zapatero cobbler

10.1 Shopping conversations

Where can I get...?	¿Dónde puedo conseguir...?
	dohndeh pwehdoh kohnsehgheer...?
When does this shop open?	¿De qué hora a qué hora abren?
	deh keh ohrah ah keh ohrah ahbrehn?
Could you tell me where the...department is?	¿Me podría indicar la sección de...?
	meh pohdreeah eendeekahr lah sehkthyohn deh...?
Could you help me, please? I'm looking for...	¿Podría ayudarme? Busco...
	pohdreeah ahyoodahrmeh? booskoh...
Do you sell British/American newspapers?	¿Venden periódicos británicos/americanos?
	behndehn pehryohdeekohs breetahneekohs/ahmehreekahnohs?

👉 ¿Lo/la atienden? _____ Are you being served?

No, I'd like...	No. Quisiera...
	noh. keesyehrah...
I'm just looking, if that's all right	Sólo estoy mirando, gracias
	sohloh ehstoy meerahndoh, grahthyahs

👉 ¿Algo más? _____ Anything else?

Yes, I'd also like...	Sí, también déme...
	see, tahmbyehn dehmeh...
No, thank you. That's all	No, gracias. Es todo
	noh, grahthyahs, ehs tohdoh
Could you show me...?	¿Me podría mostrar...?
	meh pohdreeah mohstrahr...?
I'd prefer...	Prefiero...
	prehfyehroh...
This is not what I'm looking for	No es lo que busco
	noh ehs loh keh booskoh
Thank you. I'll keep looking	Gracias. Voy a seguir mirando
	grahthyahs. boy ah sehgheer meerahndoh
Do you have something...?	¿No tendría algo ...?
	noh tehndreeah ahlgoh ...?
– less expensive?	¿No tendría algo más barato?
	noh tehndreeah ahlgoh mahs bahrahtoh?
– smaller?	¿No tendría algo más pequeño?
	noh tehndreeah ahlgoh mahs pehkehnyoh?
– larger?	¿No tendría algo más grande?
	noh tehndreeah ahlgoh mahs grahndeh?
I'll take this one	Me llevo éste/ésta
	meh lyehboh ehsteh/ehstah
Does it come with instructions?	¿Viene con instrucciones?
	byehneh kohn eenstrookthyohnehs?
It's too expensive	Me parece muy caro
	meh pahrehtheh mwee kahroh

I'll give you... _____ Le doy...
leh doy...

Could you keep this for ____ ¿Me lo/la podría guardar? Volveré más
me? I'll come back for it tarde a buscarlo
later *meh loh/lah pohdreeah gwahrdahr?*
bohlbehreh mahs tahrdeh ah booskahrloh

Have you got a bag _____ ¿Tendría una bolsita?
for me, please? *tehndreeah oonah bohlseetah?*

Could you giftwrap_____ ¿Me lo podría envolver para regalo?
it, please? *meh loh pohdreeah ehnbohlbehr pahrah*
rehgahloh?

Lo siento; no lo tenemos _____ I'm sorry, we don't have
that

Lo siento; ya no queda _____ I'm sorry, we're sold out

Lo siento, hasta el...no lo _____ I'm sorry, that won't be in
tendremos until...

Pague en la caja, por favor _____ You can pay at the cash
desk

No aceptamos tarjetas de crédito _____ We don't accept credit
cards

No aceptamos cheques de viajero _____ We don't accept traveller's
cheques

No aceptamos moneda extranjera _____ We don't accept foreign
currency

⑩ .2 Food

I'd like a hundred_____ Quisiera cien gramos de...
grams of..., please *keesyehrah thyehn grahmohs deh...*

– half a kilo of... _____ Quisiera medio kilo de...
keesyehrah mehdyoh keeloh deh...

– a kilo of... _____ Quisiera un kilo de...
keesyehrah oon keeloh deh...

Could you...it for me, _____ ¿Me lo podría...?
please? *meh loh pohdreeah...?*

Could you slice it/ _____ ¿Me lo podría cortar en lonchas/en
dice it for me, please? trozos?
meh loh pohdreeah kohrtahr ehn
lohnchahs/ehn trohthohs?

Could you grate it _____ ¿Me lo podría rallar?
for me, please? *meh loh pohdreeah rahlyahr?*

Can I order it?_____ ¿Se lo podría encargar?
seh loh pohdreeah ehnkahrgahr?

I'll pick it up tomorrow/ ____ Pasaré a buscarlo mañana/a las...
at... *pahsahreh ah booskahrloh mahnyahnah/ah*
lahs...

Can you eat/drink this? ____ ¿Es para comer/beber?
ehs pahrah kohmehr/behbehr?

What's in it? _____ ¿Qué lleva dentro?
keh lyehbah dehntroh?

I saw something in the ___ window. Shall I point it out?	He visto algo en el escaparate. ¿Se lo enseño? *eh beestoh ahlgoh ehn ehl ehskahpahrahteh, seh loh ehnsehnyoh?*
I'd like something to ___ go with this	Busco algo que haga juego con esto *booskoh ahlgoh keh ahgah <u>h</u>wehgoh kohn ehstoh*
Do you have shoes ___ in this colour?	¿Tiene zapatos de este color? *tyehneh thahpahtohs deh ehsteh kohlohr?*
I'm a size...in the UK___	En el Reino Unido tengo el número... *ehn ehl reheenoh ooneedoh tehngoh ehl noomehroh...*
Can I try this on? ___	¿Me lo podría probar? *meh loh pohdreeah prohbahr?*
Where's the fitting___ room?	¿Dónde está el probador? *dohndeh ehstah ehl prohbahdohr?*
It doesn't fit___	No me vale *noh meh bahleh*
This is the right size ___	Este es mi número *ehsteh ehs mee noomehroh*
It doesn't suit me___	No me está bien *noh meh ehstah byehn*
Do you have this/ ___ these in...?	¿Tiene éste/ésta, pero en...? *tyehneh ehsteh/ehstah pehroh ehn...?*
The heel's too high/low ___	El tacón me parece muy alto/bajo *ehl tahkohn meh pahrehtheh mwee ahltoh/bah<u>h</u>oh*
Is this/are these ___ genuine leather?	¿Es/son de piel auténtica? *ehs/sohn deh pyehl ah-ootehnteekah?*
I'm looking for a... ___ for a...-year-old baby/child	Busco un/una...para un bebé/niño de...años *booskoh oon/oonah...pahrah oon behbeh/neenyoh deh...ahnyohs*
I'd like a... ... ___	Quisiera un/una...de... *keesyehrah oon/oonah...deh...*
– silk ___	Quisiera un/una...de seda *keesyehrah oon/oonah...deh sehdah*
– cotton ___	Quisiera un/una...de algodón *keesyehrah oon/oonah...deh ahlgohdohn*
– woollen ___	Quisiera un/una...de lana *keesyehrah oon/oonah...deh lahnah*
– linen___	Quisiera un/una...de hilo *keesyehrah oon/oonah...deh eeloh*
What temperature___ can I wash it at?	¿A qué temperatura lo puedo lavar? *ah keh tehmpehrahtoorah loh pwehdoh lahbahr?*
Will it shrink in the ___ wash?	¿Encoge al lavarlo? *enkoh<u>h</u>eh ahl lahbahrloh?*

| No planchar
Do not iron | Colgar mojado
Drip dry | Lavado a mano
Hand wash |
| No centrifugar
Do not spin dry | Lavado en seco
Dry clean | Lavado a máquina
Machine wash |

10 Shopping

At the cobbler

Could you mend _____ these shoes?	¿Podría arreglar estos zapatos?
	pohdreeah ahrrehglahr ehstohs thahpahtohs?
Could you put new _____ soles/heels on these?	¿Podría ponerle nuevas suelas/nuevos tacones?
	pohdreeah pohnehrleh nwehbahs swehlahs/nwehbohs tahkohnehs?
When will they be _____ ready?	¿Para cuándo van a estar?
	pahrah kwahndoh bahn ah ehstahr?
I'd like..., please _____	Quisiera..., por favor
	keesyehrah..., pohr fahbohr
– a tin of shoe polish _____	Quisiera una crema para zapatos
	keesyehrah oonah krehmah pahrah thahpahtohs
– a pair of shoelaces_____	Quisiera un par de cordones
	keesyehrah oon pahr deh kohrdohnehs

🔟.4 Photographs and video

I'd like a film for this_____ camera, please	Quisiera un rollo/carrete para esta cámara
	keesyehrah oon rohlyoh/kahrrehteh pahrah ehstah kahmahrah
– a 126 cartridge _____	Quisiera una película en cassette de 126
	keesyehrah oonah pehleekoolah ehn kahseht deh thyehntoh beheenteesehees
– a 35mm colour slide _____	Un carrete de 35mm para diapositivas en color
	oon kahrrehteh deh treyntah ee theenkoh meeleemehtrohs pahrah deeapohseeteebahs ehn kohlohr
– a 35mm colour _____ print	Un carrete de 35mm en color
	oon kahrrehteh deh treyntah ee theenkoh meeleemehtrohs ehn kohlohr
– a 35mm black _____ and white	Un carrete de 35mm en blanco y negro
	oon kahrrehteh deh treyntah ee theenkoh meeleemehtrohs ehn blahnkoh ee nehgroh
– a videotape _____	Quisiera una cinta de vídeo
	keesyehrah oonah theentah deh veedehoh
colour/black and white_____	color/blanco y negro
	kohlohr/blahnkoh ee nehgroh
super eight _____	superocho
	soopehrohchoh
12/24/36 exposures _____	doce/veinticuatro/treinta y seis fotos
	dohtheh/beheenteekwahtroh/treheentah ee sehees fohtohs
ASA/DIN number_____	valor ISO
	bahlohr eesoh
daylight film _____	película para luz natural
	pehleekoolah pahrah looth nahtoorahl
film for artificial light _____	película para luz artificial
	pehleekoolah pahrah looth ahrteefeethyahl

Shopping

🔟

Problems

Could you load the _____ ¿Me podría poner el rollo/carrete en la
film for me, please? cámara?
meh pohdreeah pohnehr ehl
rohlyoh/kahrrehteh ehn lah kahmahrah?

Could you take the film _____ ¿Me podría sacar el rollo/carrete de la
out for me, please? cámara?
meh pohdreeah sahkahr ehl
rohlyoh/kahrrehteh deh lah kahmahrah?

Should I replace_____ ¿Tengo que cambiar las pilas?
the batteries? *tehngoh keh kahmbyahr lahs peelahs?*

Could you have a look_____ ¿Me podría revisar la cámara? Ya no
at my camera, please? funciona
It's not working *meh pohdreeah rehbeesahr lah kahmahrah?*
yah noh foonthyohnah

The...is broken _____ Está estropeado el...
ehstah ehstrohpehahdoh ehl...

The film's jammed _____ Se ha atascado el rollo/carrete
seh ah ahtahskahdoh ehl rohlyoh
/kahrrehteh

The film's broken_____ Se ha roto el rollo/carrete
seh ah rohtoh ehl rohlyoh/kahrrehteh

The flash isn't working _____ No funciona el flash
noh foonthyohnah ehl flahsh

Processing and prints

I'd like to have this film _____ Quisiera mandar a revelar/copiar este
developed/printed, rollo/carrete
please *keesyehrah mahndahr ah*
rehbehlahr/kohpyahr ehsteh
rohlyoh/kahrrehteh

I'd like...prints from_____ Quisiera...copias de cada negativo
each negative *keesyehrah...kohpyahs deh kahdah*
nehgahteeboh

glossy/mat_____ brillante/mate
breelyahnte/mahteh

I'd like to reorder_____ Quisiera encargar más copias de
these photos estas fotos
keesyehrah ehnkahrgahr mahs kohpyahs deh
ehstahs fohtohs

I'd like to have this _____ Quisiera una ampliación de esta foto
photo enlarged *keesyehrah oonah ahmplyahthyohn deh*
ehstah fohtoh

How much is_____ ¿Cuánto sale el revelado?
processing? *kwahntoh sahleh ehl rehbehlahdoh?*

– printing? _____ ¿Cuánto sale el copiado?
kwahntoh sahleh ehl kohpyahdoh?

– extra copies? _____ ¿Cuánto salen las copias adicionales?
kwahntoh sahlehn lahs kohpyahs
ahdeethyohnahlehs?

– the enlargement? _____ ¿Cuánto sale la ampliación?
kwahntoh sahleh lah ahmplyahthyohn?

When will they_____ ¿Para cuándo van a estar?
be ready? *pahrah kwahndoh bahn ah ehstahr?*

Do I have to make an _____ appointment?	¿Tengo que pedir hora? *tehngoh keh pehdeer ohrah?*
Can I come in straight ____ away?	¿Podría atenderme en seguida? *pohdreeah ahtehndehrmeh ehn sehgheedah?*
How long will I have_____ to wait?	¿Cuánto tengo que esperar? *kwahntoh tehngoh keh ehspehrahr?*
I'd like a shampoo/ _____ haircut	Quisiera lavarme/cortarme el pelo *keesyehrah lahbahrmeh/kohrtahrmeh ehl pehloh*
I'd like a shampoo for ____ oily/dry hair, please	Quisiera un champú para cabello graso/seco *keesyehrah oon chahmpoo pahrah kahbehlyoh grahsoh/sehkoh*
an anti-dandruff_____ shampoo	Quisiera un champú anticaspa *keesyehrah oon chahmpoo ahnteekahspah*
– a shampoo for_____ permed/coloured hair	Quisiera un champú para cabello con permanente/teñido. *keesyehrah oon chahmpoo pahrah kahbehlyoh kohn pehrmahnehnteh/tehnyeedoh*
– a colour rinse shampoo __	Quisiera un champú color *keesyehrah oon chahmpoo kohlohr*
– a shampoo with _____ conditioner	Quisiera un champú con acondicionador *keesyehrah oon chahmpoo kohn ahkohndeethyohnahdohr*
– highlights _____	Quisiera que me hagan claritos *keesyehrah keh meh ahgahn klahreetohs*
Do you have a colour_____ chart, please?	¿Tendría una carta de colores? *tehndreeah oonah kahrtah deh kohlohrehs?*
I want to keep it the _____ same colour	Quiero conservar el mismo color *kyehroh kohnsehrbahr ehl meesmoh kohlohr*
I'd like it darker/lighter_____	Quisiera un color más oscuro/más claro *keesyehrah oon kohlohr mahs ohskooroh/mahs klahroh*
I'd like/I don't want _____ hairspray	(No) quiero fijador *(noh) kyehroh feehahdohr*
– gel_____	(No) quiero gel *(noh) kyehroh hehl*
– lotion _____	(No) quiero loción *(noh) kyehroh lohthyohn*
I'd like a short fringe _____	Quisiera el flequillo corto *keesyehrah ehl flehkeelyoh kohrtoh*
Not too short at _____ the back	No lo quisiera demasiado corto por detrás *noh loh keesyehrah dehmahsyahdoh kohrtoh pohr dehtrahs*
Not too long here _____	No lo quisiera demasiado largo aquí *noh loh keesyehrah dehmahsyahdoh lahrgoh ahkee*
I'd like/I don't want _____ (many) curls	(No) quisiera (demasiados) rizos *(noh) keesyehrah (dehmahsyadohs) reethohs*

Shopping

10

It needs a little/a lot taken off	Hay que cortar sólo un trocito/un buen trozo *ay keh kohrtahr sohloh oon trohtheetoh/oon bwehn trohthoh*
I want a completely different style	Quisiera un modelo totalmente diferente *keesyehrah oon mohdehloh tohtahlmehnteh deefehrehnteh*
I'd like it the same as...	Quisiera el pelo como... *keesyehrah ehl pehloh kohmoh...*
– as that lady's	Quisiera el pelo como esa señora *keesyehrah ehl pehloh kohmoh ehsah sehnyohrah*
– as in this photo	Quisiera el pelo como en esta foto *keesyehrah ehl pehloh kohmoh ehn ehstah fohtoh*
Could you put the drier up/down a bit?	¿Podría poner el casco más alto/bajo? *pohdreeah pohnehr ehl kahskoh mahs ahltoh/ bahhoh?*
I'd like a facial	Quisiera una máscara facial *keesyehrah oonah mahskahrah fahthyahl*
– a manicure	Quisiera que me hagan manicura *keesyehrah keh meh ahgahn mahneekoorah*
– a massage	Quisiera que me hagan masaje *keesyehrah keh meh ahgahn mahsahheh*
Could you trim my fringe?	¿Me podría recortar el flequillo? *meh pohdreeah rehkohrtahr ehl flehkeelyoh?*
– my beard?	¿Me podría recortar la barba? *meh pohdreeah rehkohrtahr lah bahrbah?*
– my moustache?	¿Me podría recortar el bigote? *meh pohdreeah rehkohrtahr ehl beegohteh?*
I'd like a shave, please	Aféiteme, por favor *ahfeheetehmeh, pohr fahbohr*
I'd like a wet shave, please	Aféiteme a navaja, por favor *ahfeheetehmeh ah nahbahhah, pohr fahbohr*

¿Cómo quiere el corte de pelo?	How do you want it cut?
¿Qué modelo deseaba?	What style did you have in mind?
¿Qué color quiere?	What colour do you want it?
¿Esta temperatura le va bien?	Is the temperature all right for you?
¿Quiere algo para leer?	Would you like something to read?
¿Quiere algo para beber?	Would you like a drink?
¿Así está bien?	Is this what you had in mind?

At the Tourist Information Centre

11 **At** the Tourist Information Centre

11 .1 **P**laces of interest

Where's the Tourist Information, please?	¿Dónde está la oficina de turismo? *dohndeh ehstah lah ohfeetheenah deh tooreesmoh?*
Do you have a city map?	¿Tendría un plano de la ciudad? *tehndreeah oon plahnoh deh lah thyoodahdh?*
Where is the museum?	¿Dónde está el museo? *dohndeh ehstah ehl moosehoh?*
Where can I find a church?	¿Dónde podría encontrar una iglesia? *dohndeh pohdreeah ehnkohntrahr oonah eeglehsyah?*
Could you give me some information about...?	¿Me podría dar información sobre...? *meh pohdreeah dahr eenfohrmahthyohn sohbreh...?*
How much is that?	¿Cuánto le debemos por esto? *kwahntoh leh dehbehmohs pohr ehstoh?*
What are the main places of interest?	¿Cuáles son los sitios más interesantes para visitar? *kwahlehs sohn lohs seetyohs mahs eentehrehsahntehs pahrah veeseetahr?*
Could you point them out on the map?	¿Me los podría señalar en el plano? *meh lohs pohdreeah sehnyahlahr ehn ehl plahnoh?*
What do you recommend?	¿Qué nos recomienda? *keh nohs rehkohmyehndah?*
We'll be here for a few hours	Pensamos quedarnos unas horas *pehnsahmohs kehdahrnohs oonahs ohrahs*
– a day	Pensamos quedarnos un día *pehnsahmohs kehdahrnohs oon deeah*
– a week	Pensamos quedarnos una semana *pehnsahmohs kehdahrnohs oonah sehmahnah*
We're interested in...	Nos interesa... *nohs eentehrehsah...*
Is there a scenic walk around the city?	¿Hay algún circuito turístico para visitar la ciudad a pie? *ay ahlgoon theerkweetoh tooreesteekoh pahrah veeseetar lah thyoodahdh ah pyeh?*
How long does it take?	¿Cuánto dura? *kwahntoh doorah?*
Where does it start/end?	¿De dónde sale?/¿Dónde termina? *deh dohndeh sahleh?/dohndeh tehrmeenah?*
Are there any boat cruises here?	¿Hay excursiones en barco? *ay ehxkoorsyohnehs ehn bahrkoh?*
Where can we board?	¿Dónde se puede embarcar? *dohndeh seh pwehdeh ehmbahrkahr?*
Are there any bus tours?	¿Hay excursiones en autocar? *ay ehxkoorsyohnehs ehn ahootohkahr?*
Where do we get on?	¿De dónde salen? *deh dohndeh sahlehn?*
Is there a guide who speaks English?	¿Hay algún guía que hable inglés? *ay ahlgoon gheeah keh ahbleh eenglehs?*

What trips can we take ____ around the area?	¿Qué excursiones se pueden hacer en los alrededores?
	keh ehxkoorsyohnehs seh pwehdehn ahthehr ehn lohs ahlrehdehdohrehs?
Are there any _____ excursions?	¿Hay excursiones organizadas?
	ay ehxkoorsyohnehs ohrgahneethahdahs?
Where do they go to? ____	¿Hacia dónde van?
	ahthyah dohndeh bahn?
We'd like to go to..._____	Quisiéramos ir a...
	keesyehrahmohs eer ah...
How long is the trip? _____	¿Cuánto se tarda en llegar?
	kwahntoh seh tahrdah ehn lyehgahr?
How long do we _____ stay in...?	¿Cuánto dura la visita a...?
	kwahntoh doorah lah beeseetah ah...
Are there any guided _____ tours?	¿Hay visitas guiadas?
	ay beeseetahs gheeahdahs?
How much free time_____ will we have there?	¿Cuánto tiempo libre tenemos allí?
	kwahntoh tyehmpoh leebreh tehnehmohs alyee?
We want to go hiking_____	Nos gustaría hacer una excursión a pie
	nohs goostahreeah ahthehr oonah ehxkoorsyohn ah pyeh
Can we hire a guide? _____	¿Es posible contratar un guía?
	ehs pohseebleh kohntrahtahr oon gheeah?
Can I book mountain _____ huts?	¿Se puede hacer una reserva para un refugio (en la montaña)?
	seh pwehdeh ahthehr oonah rehsehrbah pahrah oon rehfoohyoh (ehn lah mohntahnyah)?
What time does... _____ open/close?	¿A qué hora abre/cierra...?
	ah keh ohrah ahbreh/thyehrrah...?
What days is...open/_____ closed?	¿Qué días tiene abierto/cerrado...?
	keh deeahs tyehneh ahbyehrtoh/thehrrahdoh...?
What's the admission_____ price?	¿Cuánto sale la entrada?
	kwahntoh sahleh lah ehntrahdah?
Is there a group _____ discount?	¿Hay descuento para grupos?
	ay dehskwehntoh pahrah groopohs?
Is there a child _____ discount?	¿Hay descuento para niños?
	ay dehskwehntoh pahrah neenyohs?
Is there a discount_____ for pensioners?	¿Hay descuento para jubilados?
	ay dehskwehntoh pahrah hoobeelahdohs?
Can I take (flash) _____ photos/can I film here?	¿Se pueden sacar fotos (con flash)/filmar aquí?
	seh pwehdehn sahkahr fohtohs(kohn flahsh)/feelmahr ahkee?
Do you have any _____ postcards of...?	¿Venden postales de...?
	behndehn pohstahlehs deh...?
Do you have an _____ English...?	¿Tiene un...en inglés?
	tyehneh oon...ehn eenglehs?
– an English catalogue?____	¿Tiene un catálogo en inglés?
	tyehneh oon kahtahlohgoh ehn eenglehs?
– an English programme?__	¿Tiene un programa en inglés?
	tyehneh oon prohgrahmah ehn eenglehs?
– an English brochure? ____	¿Tiene un folleto en inglés?
	tyehneh oon fohlyehtoh ehn eenglehs?

11 .2 Going out

● **At the cinema** most films are dubbed in Spanish. Sometimes there are only two showings, in the evening, at 7 and 11pm. In this case advance booking is advisable.

Do you have this _____
week's/month's
entertainment guide?

¿Tiene la guía de los espectáculos de esta semana/este mes?
tyehneh lah gheeah deh lohs ehspehktahkoolohs deh ehstah sehmahnah/ehsteh mehs?

What's on tonight? _____

¿Adónde podríamos ir esta noche?
ahdohndeh pohdreeahmohs eer ehstah nohcheh?

We want to go to... _____

Nos gustaría ir a...
nohs goostahreeah eer ah...

Which films are _____
showing?

¿Qué películas dan?
keh pehleekoolahs dahn?

What sort of film is that?___

¿Qué clase de película es?
keh klahseh deh pehleekoolah ehs?

suitable for everyone _____

para todos los públicos
pahrah tohdohs lohs poobleekohs

not suitable for_____
children

prohibido para menores de 12/16 años
proheebeedoh pahrah mehnohrehs deh dohtheh/dyehtheesehees ahnyohs

original version _____

versión original
behrsyohn ohree<u>h</u>eenahl

subtitled_____

subtitulada
soobteetoolahdah

dubbed_____

doblada
dohblahdah

Is it a continuous_____
showing?

¿Es sesión continua?
ehs sehsyohn kohnteenooah?

What's on at...? _____

¿Qué dan en...?
keh dahn ehn...?

– the theatre? _____

¿Qué dan en el teatro?
keh dahn ehn ehl tehahtroh?

– the concert hall?_____

¿Qué dan en la sala de conciertos?
keh dahn ehn lah sahlah deh kohnthyehrtohs?

– the opera? _____

¿Qué dan en la ópera?
keh dahn ehn lah ohpehrah?

Where can I find a good ___
disco around here?

¿Dónde hay una buena discoteca por aquí?
dohndeh ay oonah bwehnah deeskohtehkah pohr ahkee?

Is it for members only? ___

¿Hay que ser socio?
ay keh sehr sohthyoh?

Where can I find a good ___
cabaret club around
here?

¿Dónde hay un buen cabaret por aquí?
dohndeh ay oon bwehn kahbahreh pohr ahkee?

Is it evening wear only? ___

¿Hay que ir en traje de etiqueta?
ay keh eer ehn trah<u>h</u>eh deh ehteekehtah?

Is there a life guard on duty here?	¿Hay algún vigilante de servicio? *ay ahlgoon veeheelante deh sehrbeetheeoh?*
Are dogs allowed here?	¿Está permitido traer perros? *ehstah pehrmeeteedoh trahehr pehrrohs?*
Is camping on the beach allowed?	¿Está permitido acampar en la playa? *ehstah pehrmeeteedoh ahkahmpahr ehn lah plahyah?*
Are we allowed to build a fire here?	¿Está permitido hacer fuego? *ehstah pehrmeeteedoh ahthehr fwehgoh?*

Peligro **Danger**	Prohibido pescar **No fishing**	Prohibido bañarse **No swimming**
Aguas de pesca **Fishing water**	Prohibido hacer surfing **No surfing**	Permiso obligatorio **Permits only**

12.3 In the snow

Can I take ski lessons here?	¿Dan clases de esquí? *dahn klahsehs deh eskee?*
for beginners/advanced	para principiantes/avanzados *pahrah preentheepyahntehs/ahbahnthahdohs*
How large are the groups?	¿De cuántas personas son los grupos? *deh kwahntahs pehrsohnahs sohn lohs groopohs?*
What language are the classes in?	¿En qué idioma son las clases? *ehn keh eedyohmah sohn lahs klahsehs?*
I'd like a lift pass, please	Quisiera un pase para las telesillas *keesyehrah oon pahseh pahrah lahs tehlehseelyahs*
Must I give you a passport photo?	¿Se necesita foto? *seh nehthehseetah fohtoh?*
Where can I have a passport photo taken?	¿Dónde puedo sacarme fotos? *dohndeh pwehdoh sahkahrmeh fohtohs?*
Where are the beginners' slopes?	¿Dónde están las pistas para principiantes? *dohndeh ehstahn lahs peestahs pahrah preentheepyahntehs?*
Are there any runs for cross-country skiing?	¿Hay pistas de esquí de fondo por aquí? *ay peestahs deh ehskee deh fohndoh pohr ahkee?*
Have the cross-country runs been marked?	¿Las pistas de esquí de fondo están señalizadas? *lahs peestahs deh ehskee deh fohndoh ehstahn sehnyahleethahdahs?*
Are the...in operation?	¿Están abiertos los...? *ehstahn ahbyehrtohs lohs...?*
– the ski lifts	¿Ya funcionan los telesquís? *yah foonthyohnahn lohs tehlehskees?*
– the chair lifts	¿Ya funcionan las telesillas? *yah foonthyohnahn lahs tehlehseelyahs?*
Are the slopes usable?	¿Están abiertas las pistas? *ehstahn ahbyehrtahs lahs peestahs?*

Sports

12

Sickness

🔢 **S**ickness

🔢 .1 **C**all (fetch) the doctor

Could you call/fetch a_____ doctor quickly, please?	¿Podría llamar/ir a buscar rápido a un médico, por favor?
	pohdreeah lyahmahr/eer ah booskahr rahpeedoh ah oon mehdeekoh, pohr fahbohr?
When does the doctor _____ have surgery?	¿Cuándo tiene consulta el médico?
	kwahndoh tyehneh kohnsooltah ehl mehdeekoh?
When can the doctor _____ come?	¿Cuándo puede venir el médico?
	kwahndoh pwehdeh behneer ehl mehdeekoh?
I'd like to make an_____ appointment to see the doctor	¿Podría pedirme hora con el médico?
	pohdreeah pehdeermeh ohrah kohn ehl mehdeekoh?
I've got an appointment ___ to see the doctor at...	Tengo hora con el médico para las...
	tehngoh ohrah kohn ehl mehdeekoh pahrah lahs...
Which doctor/chemist _____ has night/weekend duty?	¿Qué médico/farmacia está de guardia esta noche/este fin de semana?
	keh mehdeekoh/fahrmahthyah ehstah deh gwahrdyah ehstah nohcheh/ehsteh feen deh sehmahnah?

🔢 .2 **P**atient's ailments

I don't feel well _____	No me siento bien
	noh meh syehntoh byehn
I'm dizzy_____	Tengo mareos
	tehngoh mahrehohs
– ill_____	Estoy enfermo
	ehstoy ehnfehrmoh
– sick_____	Tengo náuseas
	tehngoh nahoosehahs
I've got a cold_____	Estoy acatarrado
	ehstoy ahkahtahrrahdoh
It hurts here _____	Me duele aquí
	meh dwehleh ahkee
I've been throwing up _____	He devuelto
	eh dehbwehltoh
I've got... _____	Tengo molestias de...
	tehngoh mohlehstyahs deh...
I'm running a _____ temperature of...degrees	Tengo...grados de fiebre
	tehngoh...grahdohs deh fyehbreh
I've been stung by_____ a wasp	Me ha picado una avispa
	meh ah peekahdoh oonah ahbeespah
I've been stung by an_____ insect	Me ha picado un insecto
	meh ah peekahdoh oon eensehktoh
I've been bitten by _____ a dog	Me ha mordido un perro
	meh ah mohrdeedoh oon pehrroh
I've been stung by_____ a jellyfish	Me ha picado una medusa
	meh ah peekahdoh oonah mehdoosah

I've been bitten by _____ a snake	Me ha mordido una serpiente
	meh ah mohrdeedoh oonah sehrpyehnteh
I've been bitten by _____ an animal	Me ha picado un insecto
	meh ah peekahdoh oon eensehktoh
I've cut myself _____	Me he cortado
	meh eh kohrtahdoh
I've burned myself _____	Me he quemado
	meh eh kehmahdoh
I've grazed myself_____	Tengo una rozadura
	tehngoh oonah rohthahdoorah
I've had a fall _____	Me he caído
	meh eh kaheedoh
I've sprained my ankle_____	Me he torcido el tobillo
	meh eh tohrtheedoh ehl tohbeelyoh
I've come for the _____ morning-after pill	Vengo a que me dé una píldora del día después
	behngoh ah keh meh deh oonah peeldohrah dehl deeah dehspwehs

🤝 .3 The consultation

¿Qué molestias tiene? _____	What seems to be the problem?
¿Cuánto hace que tiene estas _____ molestias?	How long have you had these symptoms?
¿Ha tenido estas molestias _____ anteriormente?	Have you had this trouble before?
¿Qué temperatura tiene? _____	How high is your temperature?
Desnúdese._____	Get undressed, please
Desvístase de la cintura para arriba _____	Strip to the waist, please
Allí puede quitarse la ropa_____	You can undress there
Descúbrase el brazo_____ izquierdo/derecho	Roll up your left/right sleeve, please
Recuéstese aquí _____	Lie down here, please
¿Le duele esto? _____	Does this hurt?
Respire hondo_____	Breathe deeply
Abra la boca_____	Open your mouth

Patient's medical history

I'm a diabetic _____	Soy diabético
	soy deeahbehteekoh
I have a heart condition____	Soy enfermo cardíaco
	soy ehnfehrmoh kahrdeeahkoh
I have asthma_____	Soy asmático
	soy ahsmahteekoh
I'm allergic to... _____	Soy alérgico a...
	soy ahlehr<u>h</u>eekoh ah...
I'm...months pregnant _____	Estoy embarazada de...meses
	ehstoy ehmbahrahthadah deh...mehsehs
I'm on a diet _____	Sigo una dieta
	seegoh oonah dyehtah

I'm on medication/ _____ the pill	Tomo medicamentos/la píldora
	tohmoh mehdeekahmehntohs/lah peeldohrah
I've had a heart attack _____ once before	He tenido un ataque cardíaco anteriormente
	eh tehneedoh oon ahtahkeh kahrdeeahkoh ahntehryohrmehnteh
I've had a(n)...operation ___	Me han operado del/de la...
	meh ahn ohpehrahdoh dehl/deh lah...
I've been ill recently _____	He estado enfermo hace poco
	eh ehstahdoh ehnfehrmoh ahtheh pohkoh
I've got an ulcer_____	Tengo una úlcera
	tehngoh oonah oolthehrah
I've got my period_____	Tengo la regla
	tehngoh lah rehglah

¿Padece alguna alergia?_____	Do you have any allergies?
¿Toma medicamentos?_____	Are you on any medication?
¿Sigue alguna dieta?_____	Are you on a diet?
¿Está embarazada?_____	Are you pregnant?
¿Está vacunado/a contra el tétanos?_____	Have you had a tetanus injection?

The diagnosis

No es nada grave_____	It's nothing serious
Se ha fracturado el/la..._____	Your...is broken
Se ha contusionado el/la..._____	You've got a/some bruised...
Se ha desgarrado el/la..._____	You've got (a) torn...
Tiene una inflamación_____	You've got an inflammation
Tiene apendicitis_____	You've got appendicitis
Tiene bronquitis_____	You've got bronchitis
Tiene una enfermedad venérea_____	You've got a venereal disease
Tiene gripe_____	You've got the flu
Ha tenido un ataque al corazón_____	You've had a heart attack
Tiene una infección virósica/_____ bacteriana	You've got an infection (viral..., bacterial...)
Tiene una pulmonía_____	You've got pneumonia
Tiene una úlcera_____	You've got an ulcer
Se ha distendido un músculo_____	You've pulled a muscle
Tiene una infección vaginal_____	You've got a vaginal infection
Tiene una intoxicación alimenticia_____	You've got food poisoning

Tiene una insolación _____	You've got sunstroke
Es alérgico a... _____	You're allergic to...
Está embarazada _____	You're pregnant
Quisiera hacerle un análisis de sangre/de orina/de materia fecal	I'd like to have your blood/urine/stools tested
Hay que suturar la herida_____	It needs stitching
Lo/la voy a derivar a un especialista/a __ un hospital	I'm referring you to a specialist/sending you to hospital
Tiene que hacerse radiografías _____	You'll need to have some x-rays taken
Vuelva a tomar asiento en la sala de ___ espera	Could you wait in the waiting room, please?
Hay que operarlo/operarla_____	You'll need an operation

Is it contagious?_____	¿Es contagioso?
	ehs kohntahhyohsoh?
How long do I have to _____ stay...?	¿Hasta cuándo tengo que...?
	ahstah kwahndoh tehngoh keh...?
– in bed _____	¿Hasta cuándo tengo que guardar cama?
	ahstah kwahndoh tehngoh keh gwahrdahr kahmah?
– in hospital _____	¿Hasta cuándo tengo que quedarme en el hospital?
	ahstah kwahndoh tehngoh keh kehdahrmeh ehn ehl ohspeetahl?
Do I have to go on _____ a special diet?	¿Tengo que seguir alguna dieta?
	tehngoh keh sehgheer ahlgoonah dyehtah?
Am I allowed to travel? ___	¿Puedo viajar?
	pwehdoh byahhahr?
Can I make a new _____ appointment?	¿Puedo volver a pedir hora?
	pwehdoh bohlbehr ah pehdeer ohrah?
When do I have to_____ come back?	¿Cuándo tengo que volver?
	kwahndoh tehngoh keh bohlbehr?
I'll come back _____ tomorrow	Vuelvo mañana
	bwehlboh mahnyahnah

Vuelva mañana/dentro de...días _____	Come back tomorrow/in...days' time

13 .4 Medication and prescriptions

How do I take this _____ medicine?	¿Cómo se toman estos medicamentos?
	kohmoh seh tohmahn ehstohs mehdeekahmehntohs?
How many capsules/ _____ drops/injections/ spoonfuls/tablets each time?	¿Cuántas cápsulas/gotas/inyecciones/ cucharadas/tabletas por vez?
	kwahntahs kahpsoolahs/gohtahs/eenyehkthyohnehs/koo chahrahdahs pohr behth?

How many times a day? ___	¿Cuántas veces al día?
	kwahntahs behthehs ahl deeah?
I've forgotten my_____	Se me ha olvidado traer los
medication. At home I	medicamentos. En casa tomo...
take...	*seh meh ah olbeedahdoh trahehr lohs*
	mehdeekahmehntohs. ehn kahsah tohmoh...
Could you make out a _____	¿Podría hacerme una receta?
prescription for me?	*pohdreeah ahthehrmeh oonah rehthehtah?*

Voy a recetarle unos antibióticos/un_____	I'm prescribing
jarabe/un calmante/ unos	antibiotics/a mixture/a
analgésicos	tranquillizer/pain killers
Tiene que guardar reposo _____	Have lots of rest
No tiene que salir a la calle _____	Stay indoors
Tiene que guardar cama_____	Stay in bed

antes de cada	inyecciones	tragar entero
comida	injections	swallow whole
before meals	para uso externo	tabletas
cápsulas	exclusivamente	tablets
capsules	not for internal use	tomar/ingerir
diluir en agua	ungüento	take
dissolve in water	ointment	estos medicamentos
gotas	aplicar/embadurnar	afectan la capacidad
drops	rub on	de conducir
cada...horas	cucharadas (soperas/	this medication
every...hours	cucharaditas)	impairs your driving
seguir la cura hasta	spoonfuls	...vez/veces cada 24
el final	(tablespoons/	horas
finish the course	tea-spoons)	...times a day
durante...días		
for...days		

🖐 .5 At the dentist's

Do you know a good _____	¿Me podría recomendar un buen dentista?
dentist?	*meh pohdreeah rehkohmehndahr oon*
	bwehn dehnteestah?
Could you make a_____	¿Me podría pedir hora con el dentista? Es
dentist's appointment for	urgente
me? It's urgent	*meh pohdreeah pehdeer ohrah kohn ehl*
	dehnteestah? ehs oorhehnteh
Can I come in today,_____	¿Me podría atender hoy mismo?
please?	*meh pohdreeah ahtehndehr oy meesmoh?*
I have (terrible)_____	Tengo (un terrible) dolor de muelas
toothache	*tehngoh (oon tehrreebleh) dohlohr deh*
	mwehlahs
Could you prescribe/ _____	¿Me podría recetar/dar un analgésico?
give me a painkiller?	*meh pohdreeah rehthehtahr/dahr oon*
	ahnahlhehseekoh?

A piece of my tooth _____ Se me ha caído un pedazo de un diente
has broken off *seh meh ah kaheedoh oon pehdahthoh deh oon dyehnteh*

My filling's come out _____ Se me ha salido un empaste
seh meh ah sahleedoh oon ehmpahsteh

I've got a broken crown_____ Se me ha roto la corona
seh meh ah rohtoh lah kohrohnah

I'd like/I don't want a _____ Quisiera que/no quiero que me ponga
local anaesthetic anestesia local
keesyehrah keh/noh kyehroh keh meh pohngah ahnehstehsyah lohkahl

Can you do a makeshift_____ ¿Me podría hacer un arreglo provisional?
repair job? *meh pohdreeah ahthehr oon ahrrehgloh prohbeesyohnahl?*

I don't want this tooth _____ No quiero que me extraiga esta muela
pulled *noh kyehroh keh meh ehxtraygah ehstah mwehlah*

My dentures are broken. _____ Se me ha roto la dentadura postiza
Can you fix them? ¿Podría arreglármela?
seh meh ah rohtoh lah dehntahdoorah pohsteethah. pohdreeah arrehglahrmehlah?

¿Qué diente/muela le duele?_____ Which tooth hurts?
Tiene un absceso _____ You've got an abscess
Tengo que tratarle el nervio _____ I'll have to do a root canal
Voy a ponerle anestesia local _____ I'm giving you a local
anaesthetic
Tengo que empastarle/extraerle/ _____ I'll have to fill/pull this
pulirle este/esta... tooth/file this...down
Tengo que usar el torno _____ I'll have to drill
Abra la boca_____ Open wide, please
Cierre la boca_____ Close your mouth, please
Enjuáguese:_____ Rinse, please
¿Le sigue doliendo?_____ Does it hurt still?

In trouble

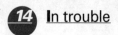

14 In trouble

14.1 Asking for help

Help!	¡Socorro!
	sohkohrroh!
Fire!	¡Fuego!
	fwehgoh!
Police!	¡Policía!
	pohleetheeah!
Quick!	¡Rápido!
	rahpeedoh!
Danger!	¡Peligro!
	pehleegroh!
Watch out!	¡Cuidado!
	kweedahdoh!
Stop!	¡Alto!
	ahltoh!
Be careful!	¡Cuidado!
	kweedahdoh!
Don't!	¡No, no!
	noh, noh!
Let go!	¡Suelte!
	swehlteh!
Stop that thief!	¡Al ladrón!
	ahl lahdrohn!
Could you help me, please?	¿Podría ayudarme, por favor?
	pohdreeah ahyoodahrmeh, pohr fahbohr?
Where's the police station/emergency exit/fire escape?	¿Dónde está la comisaría/la salida de emergencia/la escalera de incendios?
	dohndeh ehstah lah kohmeesahreeah/lah sahleedah deh ehmehrhehnthyah/lah ehskahlehrah deh eenthehndyohs?
Where's the nearest fire extinguisher?	¿Dónde hay un extintor?
	dohndeh ay oon ehksteentohr?
Call the fire brigade!	¡Llamen a los bomberos!
	lyahmehn ah lohs bohmbehrohs!
Call the police!	¡Llamen a la policía!
	lyahmehn ah lah pohleetheeah!
Call an ambulance!	¡Llamen a una ambulancia!
	lyahmehn ah oonah ahmboolahnthyah!
Where's the nearest phone?	¿Dónde hay un teléfono?
	dohndeh ay oon tehlehfohnoh?
Could I use your phone?	¿Podría llamar por teléfono?
	pohdreeah lyahmahr pohr tehlehfohnoh?
What's the emergency number?	¿Cuál es el número de urgencias?
	kwahl ehs ehl noomehroh deh oorhehnthyahs?
What's the number for the police?	¿Cuál es el número de la policía?
	kwahl ehs ehl noomehroh deh lah pohleetheeah?

14 .2 Loss

I've lost my purse/ _____ wallet	Se me ha perdido el monedero/la cartera *seh meh ah pehrdeedoh ehl mohnehdehroh/lah kahrtehrah*
I left my...behind _____ yesterday	Ayer me dejé el/la... *ahyehr meh deh<u>h</u>eh ehl/lah...*
I left my...here _____	Me he dejado el/la...aquí *meh eh deh<u>h</u>ahdoh ehl/lah...ahkee*
Did you find my...? _____	¿Han encontrado mi...? *ahn ehnkohntrahdoh mee...?*
It was right here _____	Estaba aquí *ehstahbah ahkee*
It's quite valuable _____	Es muy valioso *ehs mwee bahlyohsoh*
Where's the lost _____ property office?	¿Dónde está la oficina de objetos perdidos? *dohndeh ehstah lah ohfeetheenah deh ohb<u>h</u>ehtohs pehrdeedohs?*

14 .3 Accidents

There's been an _____ accident	Ha habido un accidente *ah ahbeedoh oon ahktheedehnteh*
Someone's fallen into _____ the water	Se ha caído alguien al agua *seh ah kaheedoh ahlgyehn ahl ahgwah*
There's a fire _____	Hay un incendio *ay oon eenthehndyoh*
Is anyone hurt? _____	¿Hay algún herido? *ay ahlgoon ehreedoh?*
Some people have _____ been/no one's been injured	(No) hay heridos *(noh) ay ehreedohs*
There's someone in _____ the car/train still	Todavía queda alguien en el coche/tren *tohdahbeeah kehdah ahlgyehn ehn ehl kohcheh/trehn*
It's not too bad. Don't _____ worry	No es grave. No se preocupe *noh ehs grahbeh. noh seh prehohkoopeh*
Leave everything the _____ way it is, please	No toque nada *noh tohkeh nahdah*
I want to talk to the _____ police first	Primero quisiera hablar con la policía *preemehroh keesyehrah ahblahr kohn lah pohleetheeah*
I want to take a _____ photo first	Primero quisiera sacar una foto *preemehroh keesyehrah sahkahr oonah fohtoh*
Here's my name _____ and address	Aquí tiene mi nombre y dirección *ahkee tyehneh mee nohmbreh ee deerehkthyohn*
Could I have your _____ name and address?	¿Me da su nombre y dirección? *meh dah soo nohmbreh ee deerehkthyohn?*
Could I see some _____ identification/your insurance papers?	¿Me permite su carnet de identidad/sus papeles del seguro? *meh pehrmeeteh soo kahrneh deh eedehnteedahdh/soos pahpehlehs dehl sehgooroh?*

In trouble

14

Will you act as a _____ witness?	¿Le importaría hacer de testigo?
	leh eempohrtahreeah ahtehr deh tehsteegoh?
I need the details for _____ the insurance	Necesito los datos para el seguro
	nehthehseetoh lohs dahtohs pahrah ehl sehgooroh
Are you insured? _____	¿Está asegurado?
	ehstah ahsehgoorahdoh?
Third party or _____ comprehensive?	¿Responsabilidad civil o contra todo riesgo?
	rehspohnsahbeeleedahdh theebeel oh kohntrah tohdoh ryehsgoh?
Could you sign here, _____ please?	Firme aquí, por favor
	feermeh ahkee, pohr fahbohr

🔴 14 .4 Theft

I've been robbed _____	Me han robado
	meh ahn rohbahdoh
My...has been stolen _____	Me han robado el/la...
	meh ahn rohbahdoh ehl/lah...
My car's been _____ broken into	Me han abierto el coche
	meh ahn ahbyehrtoh ehl kohcheh

🔴 14 .5 Missing person

I've lost my child/ _____ grandmother	Se ha perdido mi hijo/mi hija/mi abuela
	seh ah pehrdeedoh mee eehoh/mee eehah/mee ahbwehlah
Could you help me _____ find him/her?	¿Podría ayudarme a buscarlo/la?
	pohdreeah ahyoodahrmeh ah booskahrloh/lah?
Have you seen a _____ small child?	¿Ha visto a un niño pequeño/a una niña pequeña?
	ah veestoh ah oon neenyoh pehkehnyoh/ah oonah neenyah pehkehnyah?
He's/she's...years old _____	Tiene...años
	tyehneh...ahnyohs
He's/she's got _____ short/long/blond/red/ brown/black/ grey/curly/ straight/frizzy hair	Tiene el pelo corto/largo/rubio/rojo/castaño/negro/ canoso/rizado/liso/crespo
	tyehneh ehl pehloh kohrtoh/lahrgoh/roobyoh/kahstahnyoh/neh groh/kahnohsoh/reethahdoh/leesoh/krehspoh
with a ponytail _____	con cola de caballo
	kohn kohlah deh kahbahlyoh
with plaits _____	con trenzas
	kohn trehnthahs
in a bun _____	con moño
	kohn mohnyoh
He's/she's got _____ blue/brown/green eyes	Tiene ojos azules/marrones/verdes
	tyehneh ohhohs ahthoolehs/mahrrohnehs/behrdehs

He's wearing swimming ___ trunks/mountaineering boots	Lleva bañador/botas de montaña *lyehbah bahnyahdohr/bohtahs deh mohntahnyah*
with/without glasses/ _____ a bag	con/sin gafas/bolso *kohn/seen gahfahs/bohlsoh*
tall/short_____	alto/bajito *ahltoh/bahheetoh*
This is a photo of _____ him/her	Esta es su foto *ehstah ehs soo fohtoh*
He/she must be lost _____	Seguramente se habrá perdido *sehgoorahmehnteh seh ahbrah pehrdeedoh*

14 .6 The police

An arrest

Los papeles del coche, por favor_____	Your registration papers, please
Conducía demasiado rápido _____	You were speeding
Tiene mal aparcado el coche_____	You're not allowed to park here
No ha puesto monedas en el _____ parquímetro	You haven't put money in the meter
No le funcionan los faros_____	Your lights aren't working
Le vamos a poner una multa de... _____ pesetas	That's a...pesetas fine
¿Va a pagar la multa en el acto? _____	Do you want to pay on the spot?
Tiene que pagar en el acto_____	You'll have to pay on the spot

I don't speak Spanish_____	No hablo español *noh ahbloh ehspahnyohl*
I didn't see the sign _____	No he visto el cartel *noh eh beestoh ehl kahrtehl*
I don't understand_____ what it says	No entiendo lo que dice *noh ehntyehndoh loh keh deetheh*
I was only doing..._____ kilometres an hour	Sólo iba a...kilómetros por hora *sohloh eebah ah...keelohmehtrohs pohr ohrah*
I'll have my car checked ___	Haré revisar el coche *ahreh rehbeesahr ehl kohcheh*
I was blinded by _____ oncoming lights	Me cegó un coche que venía de frente *meh thehgoh oon kohcheh keh behneeah deh frehnteh*

At the police station

I want to report a_____ collision/missing person/rape	Vengo a hacer la denuncia de un choque/un extravío/una violación *behngoh ah ahthehr lah dehnoonthyah deh oon chohkeh/oon ehxtrahbeeoh/oonah beeohlahthyohn*

In trouble

14

Could you make out a report, please?	¿Podría hacer un atestado?
	pohdreeah ahtehr oon ahtehstahdoh?
Could I have a copy for the insurance?	¿Me podría dar una copia para el seguro?
	meh pohdreeah dahr oonah kohpyah pahrah ehl sehgooroh?
I've lost everything	He perdido todo
	eh pehrdeedoh tohdoh

¿Dónde ha sido?	Where did it happen?
¿Qué se le ha perdido?	What's missing?
¿Qué le han robado?	What's been taken?
¿Me permite su documento de identidad?	Could I see some identification?
¿A qué hora ocurrió?	What time did it happen?
¿Quiénes estuvieron implicados?	Who was involved?
¿Hay testigos?	Are there any witnesses?
Rellene este formulario	Fill this out, please
Firme aquí, por favor	Sign here, please
¿Quiere un intérprete?	Do you want an interpreter?

I'd like an interpreter	Quisiera un intérprete
	keesyehrah oon eentehrprehteh
I'm innocent	Soy inocente
	soy eenohthehnteh
I don't know anything about it	No sé nada
	noh seh nahdah
I want to speak to someone...	Quisiera hablar con alguien de...
	keesyehrah ahblahr kohn ahlgyehn deh...
from the British consulate	Quisiera hablar con alguien del Consulado Británico
	keesyehrah ahblahr kohn ahlgyehn dehl kohnsoolahdoh breetahneekoh
I need to see someone from the British embassy	Quisiera hablar con alguien de la Embajada Británica
	keesyehrah ahblahr kohn ahlgyehn deh lah ehmbah<u>h</u>ahdah breetahneekah
I want a lawyer who speaks English	Quisiera un abogado que hable inglés
	keesyehrah oon ahbohgahdoh keh ahbleh eenglehs

15

Word list

Word list English - Spanish

● **This word list** is meant to supplement the previous chapters. Nouns are always accompanied by the Spanish definite article in order to indicate whether it is a masculine (el) or feminine (la) word. In a number of cases, words not contained in this list can be found elsewhere in this booklet, namely alongside the diagrams of the car, the bicycle and the tent. Many food terms can be found in the Spanish-English list in 4.7.

A

a little	un poco	oon pohkoh
above (up)	arriba	ahrreebah
abroad	el extranjero	ehl ehxtrahnhehroh
accident	el accidente	ehl ahktheedehnteh
adder	la víbora	la veebohrah
addition	la suma	lah soomah
address	la dirección	lah deerehkthyohn
admission	la entrada	lah ehntrahdah
admission price	el precio de entrada	ehl prehthyoh deh lah ehntrahdah
admission ticket	la entrada	lah ehntrahdah
advice	el consejo	ehl kohnsehhoh
after	después de	dehspwehs deh
afternoon (in the)	(por) la tarde	(pohr) lah tahrdeh
aftershave	la loción para después del afeitado	lah lohthyohn pahrah dehspwehs dehl ahfehytahdoh
again	de nuevo	deh nwehboh
against	contra	kohntrah
age	la edad	lah ehdahdh
Aids	el Sida	ehl seedah
air conditioning	el aire acondicionado	ehl ayreh ahkohndeethyohnahdoh
air mattress	el colchón neumático	ehl kohlchohn nehoomahteekoh
air sickness bag	bolsita para el mareo	bohlseetah pahrah ehl mahrehoh
aircraft	el avión	ehl ahbyohn
airport	el aeropuerto	ehl ahehrohpwehrtoh
alarm	la alarma	lah ahlahrmah
alarm clock	el despertador	ehl dehspehrtahdohr
alcohol	el alcohol	ehl ahlkohohl
all the time	cada vez	kahdah behth
allergic	alérgico	ahlehrheekoh
alone	solo	sohloh
always	siempre	syehmpreh
ambulance	la ambulancia	lah ahmboolahnthyah
amount	el importe	ehl eempohrteh
amusement park	el parque de atracciones	ehl pahrkeh deh ahtrahkthyohnehs
anaesthetize	anestesiar	ahnehstehsyahr
anchovy	la anchoa	lah ahnchohah
angry	enfadado	ehnfahdahdoh
animal	el animal	ehl ahneemahl
ankle	el tobillo	ehl tohbeelyoh
answer	la respuesta	lah rehspwehstah

ant	la hormiga	*lah ohrmeegah*
antibiotics	los antibióticos	*lohs ahnteebyohteekohs*
antifreeze	el anticongelante	*ehl ahnteekohn<u>h</u>ehlahnteh*
antique	antiguo	*ahnteegwoh*
antiques	las antigüedades	*lahs ahnteegwehdahdehs*
anus	el ano	*ehl ahnoh*
apartment	el apartamento	*ehl ahpahrtahmehntoh*
aperitif	el aperitivo	*ehl ahpehreeteeboh*
apologies	las disculpas	*lahs deeskoolpahs*
apple	la manzana	*lah mahnthahnah*
apple juice	el zumo de manzana	*ehl thoomoh deh mahnthahnah*
apple pie	la tarta de manzana	*lah tahrtah deh mahnthahnah*
apple sauce	el puré de manzanas	*ehl pooreh deh mahnthahnahs*
appointment	la hora	*lah ohrah*
approximately	más o menos	*mahs oh mehnohs*
April	abril	*ahbreel*
archbishop	el arzobispo	*ehl ahrthohbeespoh*
architecture	la arquitectura	*lah ahrkeetehktoorah*
area	los alrededores	*lohs ahlrehdehdohrehs*
arm	el brazo	*ehl brahthoh*
arrange to meet	quedar	*kehdahr*
arrive	llegar	*lyehgahr*
arrow	la flecha	*lah flehchah*
art	el arte	*ehl ahrteh*
artery	la arteria	*lah ahrtehryah*
artichokes	las alcachofas	*lahs ahlkahchohfahs*
article	el artículo	*ehl ahrteekooloh*
artificial respiration	la respiración artificial	*lah rehspeerahthyohn ahrteefeethyahl*
arts and crafts	la artesanía	*lah ahrtehsahneeah*
ashtray	el cenicero	*ehl thehneethehroh*
ask (a question)	preguntar	*prehgoontahr*
ask for	pedir	*pehdeer*
asparagus	los espárragos	*lohs ehspahrrahgohs*
aspirin	la aspirina	*lah ahspeereenah*
assault	la agresión	*lah ahgrehsyohn*
aubergine	la berenjena	*lah behrehn<u>h</u>ehnah*
August	agosto	*ahgohstoh*
automatic	automático	*ahootohmahteekoh*
automatic car	el coche con cambio automático	*ehl kohcheh kohn kahmbyoh ahootohmahteekoh*
autumn	el otoño	*ehl ohtohnyoh*
avalanche	el alud	*ehl ahloodh*
awake (adj.)	despierto	*dehspyehrtoh*
awning	el toldo	*ehl tohldoh*

Word list

15

baby	el bebé	*ehl behbeh*
baby food	la comida para bebés	*lah kohmeedah pahrah behbehs*
babysitter	la niñera	*lah neenyehrah*
back (at the)	atrás	*ahtrahs*
back	la espalda	*lah ehspahldah*
backpack	la mochila	*lah mohcheelah*
bacon	el tocino	*ehl tohtheenoh*
bad	mal, malo	*mahl, mahloh*
bag	la bolsa	*lah bohlsah*
baker	la panadería	*lah pahnahdehreeah*
balcony (theatre)	el palco (alto)	*ehl pahlkoh (ahltoh)*
balcony (to building)	el balcón	*ehl bahlkohn*
ball	la pelota	*lah pehlohtah*
ballet	el ballet	*ehl bahleh*
ballpoint pen	el bolígrafo	*ehl bohleegrahfoh*
banana	el plátano	*ehl plahtahnoh*
bandage	la gasa	*lah gahsah*
bank (river)	la orilla	*lah ohreelyah*
bank	el banco	*ehl bahnkoh*
bank card	la tarjeta del banco	*lah tahrhehtah dehl bahnkoh*
bar (café)	el bar	*ehl bahr*
bar (drinks' cabinet)	la barra	*lah bahrrah*
bar	la barra	*lah bahrrah*
barbecue	la barbacoa	*lah bahrbahkohah*
basketball	el baloncesto	*ehl bahlohnthehstoh*
bath	el baño	*ehl bahnyoh*
bath attendant	el bañista	*ehl bahnyeestah*
bath foam	el gel de baño	*ehl hehl deh bahnyoh*
bath towel	la toalla de baño	*lah tohahlyah deh bahnyoh*
bathing cap	el gorro de baño	*ehl gohrroh deh bahnyoh*
bathing cubicle	la caseta	*lah kahsehtah*
bathing suit	el bañador	*ehl bahnyahdohr*
bathroom	el cuarto de baño	*ehl kwahrtoh deh bahnyoh*
battery (car)	la batería	*lah bahtehreeah*
battery	la pila	*lah peelah*
beach	la playa	*lah plahyah*
beans	las judías blancas	*lahs hoodeeahs blahnkahs*
beautiful	bonito	*bohneetoh*
beauty parlour	el salón de belleza	*ehl sahlohn deh behlyehthah*
bed	la cama	*lah kahmah*
bee	la abeja	*lah ahbehhah*
beef	la carne de vaca	*lah kahrneh deh bahkah*
beer	la cerveza	*lah thehrbehthah*
beetroot	la remolacha	*lah rehmohlahchah*
begin	empezar	*ehmpehthahr*
beginner	el principiante	*ehl preentheepyahnteh*
behind	atrás	*ahtrahs*
Belgian (f)	la belga	*lah behlgah*
Belgian (m)	el belga	*ehl behlgah*

Belgium	Bélgica	*behlheekah*
bellboy	el mozo de cuerda	*ehl mohtoh deh kwehrdah*
belt	el cinturón	*ehl theentoorohn*
berth	la litera	*lah leetehrah*
better	mejor	*mehhohr*
bicarb	el bicarbonato	*ehl beekahrbohnahtoh*
bicycle	la bicicleta	*lah beetheeklehtah*
bicycle pump	el inflador	*ehl eenflahdohr*
bicycle repairman	el mecánico de bicicletas	*ehl mehkahneekoh deh beetheeklehtahs*
bikini	el bikini	*ehl beekeenee*
bill	la cuenta	*lah kwehntah*
billiards, to play	el juego de billar	*ehl hwehgoh deh beelyahr*
birthday (to have a)	cumplir años	*koompleer ahnyohs*
birthday	el cumpleaños	*ehl koomplehahnyohs*
biscuit	la galleta	*lah gahlyehtah*
bite	morder	*mohrdehr*
bitter	amargo	*ahmahrgoh*
black	negro	*nehgroh*
bland	soso	*sohsoh*
blanket	la manta	*lah mahntah*
bleach	teñir de rubio	*tehnyeer deh roobyoh*
blister	la ampolla	*lah ahmpohlyah*
blond	rubio	*roobyoh*
blood	la sangre	*lah sahngreh*
blood pressure	la tensión sanguínea	*lah tehnsyohn sahngheenehah*
blouse	la blusa	*lah bloosah*
blow dry	secar a mano	*sehkahr ah mahnoh*
blue	azul	*ahthool*
boat	el barco	*ehl bahrkoh*
body	el cuerpo	*ehl kwehrpoh*
body milk	la leche corporal	*lah lehcheh kohrpohrahl*
boiled	cocido	*kohtheedoh*
boiled ham	el jamón de York	*ehl hahmohn deh yohrk*
bonbon	el bombón	*ehl bohmbohn*
bone	el hueso	*ehl wehsoh*
bonnet	el capó	*ehl kahpoh*
book (verb)	reservar	*rehsehrbahr*
book	el libro	*ehl leebroh*
booked	reservado	*rehsehrbahdoh*
booking office	la taquilla	*lah tahkeelyah*
bookshop	la librería	*lah leebrehreeah*
border	la frontera	*lah frohntehrah*
bored (be)	aburrirse	*ahboorreerseh*
boring	aburrido	*ahboorreedoh*
born	nacido	*nahtheedoh*
botanical gardens	el jardín botánico	*ehl hahrdeen bohtahneekoh*
both	ambos/ambas	*ahmbohs/ahmbahs*
bottle (baby's)	el biberón	*ehl beebehrohn*
bottle	la botella	*lah bohtehlyah*
bottle-warmer	el calentador de biberones	*ehl kahlehntahdohr de beebehrohnehs*
box (in theatre)	el palco	*ehl pahlkoh*

box	la caja	kahhah
boy	el chico	ehl cheekoh
bra	el sujetador	ehl soohehtahdohr
bracelet	la pulsera	lah poolsehrah
braised	estofado	ehstohfahdoh
brake	el freno	ehl frehnoh
brake fluid	el líquido de frenos	ehl leekeedoh deh frehnohs
bread	el pan	ehl pahn
bread roll	el panecillo	ehl pahnehtheelyoh
breakdown recovery	el auxilio en carretera	ehl ahooxeelyoh ehn kahrrehtehrah
break (limb)	fracturarse	frahktoorahrse
breakfast	el desayuno	ehl dehsahyoonoh
breast	el pecho	ehl pehchoh
bridge	el puente	ehl pwehnteh
bring	llevar	lyehbahr
brochure	el folleto	ehl fohlyehtoh
broken	roto, estropeado	rohtoh, ehstrohpehahdoh
broth	el caldo	ehl kahldoh
brother	el hermano	ehl ehrmahnoh
brown	marrón	mahrrohn
bruise (verb)	contusionarse	kohntoosyohnahrseh
brush	el cepillo	ehl thehpeelyoh
Brussels sprouts	las coles de Bruselas	lahs kohlehs deh broosehlahs
bucket	el cubo	ehl kooboh
bug	el bicho	ehl beechoh
building	el edificio	ehl ehdeefeethyoh
bullfight	la corrida de toros	lah kohrreedah deh tohrohs
buoy	la boya	lah boyah
burglary	el robo en una casa	ehl rohboh ehn oonah kahsah
burn (verb)	quemar	kehmahr
burn	la quemadura	lah kehmahdoorah
burnt	quemado	kehmahdoh
bus	el autobús	ehl ahootohboos
bus station	la estación de autobuses	lah ehstahthyohn deh ahootohboos
bus stop	la parada de autobús	lah pahrahdah deh ahootohboos
business class	la clase preferente	lah klahseh prehfehrehnteh
business trip	el viaje de negocios	ehl byahheh deh nehgohthyohs
busy (crowded)	hay mucha gente	ay moochah hehnteh
butane camping gas	el gas butano	ehl gahs bootahnoh
butcher's	la carnicería	lah kahrneethehreeah
butter	la mantequilla	lah mahntehkeelyah
button	el botón	ehl bohtohn
buy	comprar	kohmprahr
by airmail	el correo aéreo/vía aérea	ehl kohrrehoh ahehrehoh/beeah ahehrehah

c

cabbage	la col, la berza	*lah kohl, lah behrthah*
cabin	la cabaña	*lah kahbahnyah*
cake	el pastel	*ehl pahstehl*
cake shop	la pastelería, la confitería	*lah pahstehlehreeah, lah kohnfeetehreeah*
call (by phone)	llamar por teléfono	*lyahmahr pohr tehlehfohnoh*
called, to be	llamarse	*lyahmahrseh*
camera	la máquina fotográfica	*lah mahkeenah fohtohgrahfeekah*
camp	acampar	*ahkahmpahr*
camp shop	la tienda del camping	*lah tyehndah dehl kahmpeen*
camp site	el camping	*ehl kahmpeen*
camper van	el autocaravana	*ehl ahootohkahrah-bahnah*
campfire	la fogata	*lah fohgahtah*
camping guide	la guía de camping	*lah gheeah deh kahmpeen*
camping permit	el permiso de acampar	*ehl pehrmeesoh deh ahkahmpahr*
canal boat	el barco de excursión	*ehl bahrkoh deh ehxkoorsyohn*
cancel	cancelar	*kahnthehlahr*
candle	la vela	*lah behlah*
canoe	la piragua	*lah peerahgwah*
canoeing	el piragüismo	*ehl peerahgweesmoh*
cap (hat)	el gorro	*ehl gohrroh*
car	el coche	*ehl kohcheh*
car deck	la bodega para coches	*lah bohdehgah pahrah kohchehs*
car documents	los papeles del coche	*lohs pahpehlehs dehl kohcheh*
car registration	el permiso de circulación	*ehl pehrmeesoh deh theerkoolahthyohn*
car trouble	la avería	*lah ahbehreeah*
carafe	la jarra	*lah ḥahrrah*
caravan	la caravana	*lah kahrahbahnah*
cardigan	el chaleco	*ehl chahlehkoh*
careful	con cuidado	*kohn kweedahdoh*
carrot	la zanahoria	*lah thahnahohryah*
carton	el cartón	*ehl kahrtohn*
cartridge	el carrete de cassette	*ehl kahrrehteh deh kahseht*
cascade	la cascada	*lah kahskahdah*
cash desk	la caja	*lah kaḥḥah*
casino	el casino	*ehl kahseenoh*
cassette	la cassette	*lah kahseht*
castle	el castillo	*ehl kahsteelyoh*
cat	el gato	*ehl gahtoh*
catalogue	el catálogo	*ehl kahtahlohgoh*
cathedral	la catedral	*lah kahtehdrahl*
cauliflower	la coliflor	*lah kohleeflohr*
cave	la gruta	*lah grootah*
CD	el compact disc	*ehl kohmpahkt deesk*

Word list

15

celebrate	celebrar una fiesta	*thehlehbrahr oonah fyehsta*
cellotape	la celo	*lah thehloh*
cemetery	el cementerio	*ehl thehmehntehryoh*
centimetre	centímetro(s)	*thehnteemehtroh(s)*
central heating	la calefacción central	*lah kahlehfakthyohn thehntrahl*
centre (in the)	en el centro/ medio	*ehn ehl thehntroh/ mehdyoh*
centre	el centro	*ehl thehntroh*
chair	la silla	*lah seelyah*
chambermaid	la camarera	*lah kahmahrehrah*
chamois	la gamuza	*lah gahmoothah*
champagne	el champán/el cava	*ehl chahmpahn/ehl kahbah*
change (from paying)	la vuelta	*lah bwehltah*
change (train/plane etc.)	hacer trasbordo	*ahtehr trahsbohrdoh*
change (verb)	cambiar	*kahmbyahr*
change the baby's nappy	cambiar los pañales	*kahmbyahr lohs pahnyahlehs*
change the oil	cambiar el aceite	*kahmbyahr ehl ahtheyteh*
chapel	la capilla	*lah kahpeelyah*
charter flight	el vuelo chárter	*ehl bwehloh chahrtehr*
chat up	ligar	*leegahr*
check (verb)	controlar	*kohntrohlahr*
check in	facturar	*frahktoorahr*
cheers	salud	*sahloodh*
cheese (tasty, mild)	el queso (añejo, blando)	*ehl kehsoh (ahnyeh̲h̲oh,blahndoh)*
chef	el jefe	*ehl h̲ehfeh*
chemist	la droguería	*lah drohguehreeah*
cheque	el cheque	*ehl chehkeh*
cherries	las cerezas	*lahs thehrehthahs*
chess (play)	jugar al ajedrez	*h̲oogahr ahl ah̲ehdreth*
chewing gum	el chicle	*ehl cheekleh*
chicken	el pollo	*ehl pohlyoh*
chicory	las endivias	*lahs ehndeebyahs*
child	el hijo, el niño	*ehl eeh̲oh, ehl neenyoh*
child seat	el asiento para niños	*ehl ahsyehntoh pahrah neenyohs*
child's seat	el sillín para niños	*ehl seelyeen pahrah neenyohs*
chilled	refrigerado	*rehfreeh̲ehrahdoh*
chin	la barbilla	*lah bahrbeelyah*
chips/crisps	las patatas fritas	*lahs pahtahtahs freetahs*
chocolate	el chocolate	*ehl chohkohlahteh*
choose	elegir/escoger	*ehlehh̲eer/ehskohh̲ehr*
chop	la chuleta	*la choolehtah*
christian name	el nombre	*ehl nohmbreh*
church	la iglesia	*lah eeglehsyah*
church service	el servicio religioso	*ehl sehrbeethyoh rehleeh̲yohsoh*
cigar	el puro	*ehl pooroh*
cigar shop	el estanco	*ehl ehstahnkoh*
cigarette	el cigarrillo	*ehl theegahrreelyoh*

cigarette paper	el papel de fumar	*ehl pahpehl deh foomahr*
cine camera	la filmadora	*lah feelmahdohrah*
circle	el círculo	*ehl theerkooloh*
circus	el circo	*ehl theerkoh*
city map	el plano	*ehl plahnoh*
classic/classical	clásica	*klahseekah*
clean (adj.)	limpio	*leempyoh*
clean (verb)	limpiar	*leempyahr*
clear (adj.)	claro	*klahroh*
clearance	la liquidación	*lah leekeedahthyohn*
closed	cerrado	*thehrrahdoh*
closed off	(la carretera) cerrada	*(lah kahrrehtehrah) thehrrahdah*
clothes	la ropa	*lah rohpah*
clothes hanger	la percha	*lah pehrchah*
clothes peg	la pinza para la ropa	*lah peenthah pahrah lah rohpah*
coat	el abrigo	*ehl ahbreegoh*
cockroach	la cucaracha	*lah kookahrahchah*
cod	el bacalao (fresco)	*ehl bahkahlahoh (frehskoh)*
coffee	el café	*ehl kahfeh*
coffee creamer	la crema para el café	*lah krehmah pahrah ehl kahfeh*
coffee filter	el filtro de café	*ehl feeltroh deh kahfeh*
cognac	el coñac	*ehl kohnyah*
cold	frío	*freeoh*
cold	el constipado	*ehl kohnsteepahdoh*
cold cuts	los fiambres	*lohs fyahmbrehs*
collarbone	la clavícula	*lah klahbeekoolah*
colleague	el/la colega	*ehl/lah kohlehgah*
collision	el choque	*ehl chohkeh*
cologne	el agua de tocador	*ehl ahgwah deh tohkahdohr*
colour	el color	*ehl kohlohr*
colour TV	el televisor color	*ehl tehlehbeesohr kohlohr*
coloured pencils	los lápices de colores	*lohs lahpeethehs deh kohlohrehs*
colouring book	el libro para colorear	*ehl leebroh pahrah kohlohrehahr*
comb	el peine	*ehl peheeneh*
come	venir	*behneer*
compartment	el compartimiento	*ehl kohmpahrteemyehntoh*
complaint (medical)	la molestia	*lah mohlehstyah*
complaint	la queja	*lah kehhah*
complaints book	el libro de reclamaciones	*ehl leebroh deh rehklahmahthyohnehs*
completely	del todo	*dehl tohdoh*
compliment	el cumplido	*ehl koompleedoh*
compulsory	obligatorio	*ohbleegahtohryoh*
concert	el concierto	*ehl kohnthyehrtoh*
concert hall	la sala de conciertos	*lah sahlah deh kohnthyehrtohs*

Word list

15

concussion	la conmoción cerebral	lah kohnmohthyohn thehrehbrahl
condiments	los condimentos	lohs kohndeemehntohs
condom	el condón	ehl kohndohn
congratulate	felicitar	fehleetheetahr
connection	el enlace	ehl ehnlahtheh
constipation	el estreñimiento	ehl ehstrehnyeemyehntoh
consulate	el consulado	ehl kohnsoolahdoh
consultation	la consulta	lah kohnsooltah
contact lens	la lentilla	lah lehnteelyah
contact lens solution	el líquido para las lentillas	ehl leekeedoh pahrah lahs lehnteelyahs
contagious	contagioso	kohntahhyohsoh
contest	el concurso	ehl kohnkoorsoh
contraceptive	el anticonceptivo	ehl ahnteekohn-thehpteeboh
contraceptive pill	la píldora anticonceptiva	ah peeldohrah lahnteekohnthehpteebah
convent	el convento	ehl kohnbehntoh
cook (verb)	cocinar	kohtheenahr
cook	el cocinero	ehl kohtheenehroh
copper	el cobre	ehl kohbreh
copy	la copia	lah kohpyah
corkscrew	el sacacorchos	ehl sahkahkohrchohs
corn flour	la maicena	lah maythehnah
corner	el rincón	ehl reenkohn
correct	correcto	kohrrehktoh
correspond	cartearse	kahrtehahrseh
corridor	el pasillo	ehl pahseelyoh
costume	el traje	ehl trahheh
cot	la cuna	lah koonah
cotton	el algodón	ehl ahlgohdohn
cotton wool	el algodón	ehl ahlgohdohn
cough	la tos	lah tohs
cough mixture	el jarabe para la tos	ehl hahrahbeh pahrah lah tohs
counter	el mostrador	ehl mohstrahdohr
country	el país	ehl pahees
country code	el indicativo del país	ehl eendeekahteeboh dehl pahees
country(side)	el campo	ehl kahmpoh
courgette	el calabacín	ehl kahlahbahtheen
course (of treatment)	la cura	lah koorah
cousin (f)	la prima	lah preemah
cousin (m)	el primo	ehl preemoh
crab	el cangrejo	ehl kahngrehoh
cream	la crema, la nata	lah krehmah, lah nahtah
credit card	la tarjeta de crédito	lah tahrhehtah deh krehdeetoh
crisps/chips	las patatas fritas	lahs pahtahtahs freetahs
croissant	el croissant	ehl krwahsahn
cross the road	cruzar la calle	kroothahr lah kahlyeh
cross-country run	la pista de esquí de fondo	lah peestah deh ehskee deh fohndoh

cross-country skiing	el esquí de fondo	*ehl ehskee deh fohndoh*
cross-country skis	los esquís de fondo	*lohs ehskees deh fohndoh*
crossing (journey)	la travesía	*lah trahbehseeah*
cry (verb)	llorar	*lyohrahr*
cubic metre(s)	metro(s) cúbico(s)	*mehtroh(s) koobeekoh(s)*
cucumber	el pepino	*ehl pehpeenoh*
cuddly toy	el animal de peluche	*ehl ahneemahl deh pehloocheh*
cuff links	los gemelos	*lohs <u>h</u>ehmehlohs*
culottes	la falda-pantalón	*lah fahldah pahntahlohn*
cup	la taza	*lah tahthah*
curly	rizado	*reethahdoh*
current	la corriente	*lah kohrryehnteh*
cushion	el cojín	*ehl coh<u>h</u>een*
custard	las natillas	*lahs nahteelyahs*
customary	habitual	*ahbeetwahl*
customs	la aduana	*lah ahdwahna*
customs check	el control de aduanas	*ehl kohntrohl deh ahdwahnahs*
cut (verb)	cortar	*kohrtahr*
cutlery	los cubiertos	*lohs koobyehrtohs*
cycling	montar en bicicleta	*mohntahr ehn beetheeklehtah*

D

dairy products	los productos lácteos	*lohs prodooktohs lahktehohs*
damaged	dañado, estropeado	*dahnyahdoh, ehstrohpehahdoh*
dance	bailar	*bahylahr*
dandruff	la caspa	*lah kahspah*
danger	el peligro	*ehl pehleegroh*
dangerous	peligroso	*pehleegrohsoh*
dark	oscuro	*ohskooroh*
date	la cita	*lah theetah*
daughter	la hija	*lah ee<u>h</u>ah*
day	el día, las 24 horas	*ehl deeah, lahs beheenteekwahtroh ohrahs*
day before yesterday	anteayer	*ahntehahyehr*
dead	muerto	*mwehrtoh*
decaffeinated	sin cafeína	*seen kahfeheenah*
December	diciembre	*deethyehmbreh*
deck chair	el sillón de playa	*ehl seelyohn deh plahyah*
declare(customs)	declarar	*dehklahrahr*
deep	hondo	*ohndoh*
deep sea diving	el buceo	*ehl boothehoh*
degrees	los grados	*lohs grahdohs*
delay	el retraso	*ehl rehtrahsoh*
delicious	delicioso	*dehleethyohsoh*
dentist	el dentista	*ehl dehnteestah*
dentures	la dentadura postiza	*lah dehntahdoorah pohsteethah*

deodorant	el desodorante	*ehl dehsohdohrahnteh*
department	la sección	*lah sehkthyohn*
department stores	los grandes almacenes	*lohs grahndehs ahlmahthehnehs*
departure	la partida	*lah pahrteedah*
departure time	la hora de salida	*lah ohrah deh sahleedah*
depilatory cream	la crema depilatoria	*lah krehmah dehpeelahtohryah*
deposit (in)	en consigna	*ehn kohnseegnah*
deposit	la fianza	*lah fyahnzah*
dessert	el postre	*ehl pohstreh*
destination	el destino, el punto final	*ehl dehsteenoh, ehl poontoh feenahl*
develop (photos)	revelar	*rehbehlahr*
diabetic	el diabético	*ehl dyahbehteekoh*
dial (verb)	marcar	*mahrkahr*
diamond	el diamante	*ehl deeahmahnteh*
diarrhoea	la diarrea	*lah deeahrrehah*
dictionary	el diccionario	*ehl deekthyohnahryoh*
diesel	el gasóleo	*ehl gahsohlehoh*
diet	la dieta	*lah dyehtah*
difficulty	la dificultad	*lah deefeekooltahdh*
dining room	el comedor	*ehl kohmehdohr*
dining/buffet car	el coche restaurante	*ehl kohcheh rehstahoorahnteh*
dinner (to have)	cenar	*thehnahr*
dinner	la cena, la comida	*lah thehnah, lah kohmeedah*
dinner jacket	el smoking	*ehl smohkeen*
direction	la dirección	*lah deerehkthyohn*
directly	directo	*deerehktoh*
dirty	sucio	*soothyoh*
disabled person	el minusválido	*ehl meenoosbahleedoh*
disappearance	la desaparición	*lah dehsahpahree-thyohn*
disco	la discoteca	*lah deeskohtehkah*
discount	el descuento	*ehl dehskwehntoh*
dish	el plato	*ehl plahtoh*
dish of the day	el plato del día	*ehl plahtoh dehl deeah*
disinfectant	el desinfectante	*ehl dehseen-fehktahnteh*
distance	la distancia	*lah deestahnthyah*
distilled water	el agua destilada	*ehl ahgwah dehsteelahdah*
disturb	molestar	*mohlehstahr*
disturbance	el fallo	*ehl fahlyoh*
dive (verb)	bucear	*boothehahr*
diving	el buceo	*ehl boothehoh*
diving board	el trampolín	*ehl trahmpohleen*
diving gear	el equipo de buzo	*ehl ehkeepoh deh boothoh*
divorced	divorciado	*deebohrthyahdoh*
DIY-shop	la tienda de artículos de bricolaje	*lah tyehndah deh ahrteekoolohs deh breekohla̱heh*
dizzy	mareado	*mahrehahdoh*

do (verb)	hacer	*ahthehr*
doctor	el médico	*ehl mehdeekoh*
dog	el perro	*ehl pehrroh*
doll	la muñeca	*lah moonyehkah*
domestic	nacionales	*nahtheeohnahlehs*
done	hecho	*ehchoh*
door	la puerta	*lah pwehrtah*
double	doble	*dohbleh*
down	abajo	*ahbah̲hoh*
draught (to be a)	haber corriente	*ahbehr kohrryehnteh*
draughts (play)	jugar a las damas	*h̲oogahr ah lahs dahmahs*
dream	soñar	*sohnyahr*
dress	el vestido	*ehl behsteedoh*
dressing gown	la bata	*lah bahtah*
drink (verb)	beber	*behbehr*
drinking chocolate	el chocolate	*ehl chohkohlahteh*
drinking water	el agua potable	*ehl ahgwah pohtahbleh*
drive (verb)	ir en coche	*eer ehn kohcheh*
driver	el chófer	*ehl chohfehr*
driving licence	el permiso de conducir	*ehl pehrmeesoh deh kohndootheer*
drought	la sequía	*lah sehkeeah*
dry (verb)	secar	*sehkahr*
dry	seco	*sehkoh*
dry clean	lavar en seco	*lahbahr ehn sehkoh*
dry cleaner's	la tintorería	*lah teentohrehreeah*
dry shampoo	el champú seco	*ehl chahmpoo sehkoh*
dummy	el chupete	*ehl choopehteh*
during	durante	*doorahnteh*
during the day	de día	*deh deeah*

E

ear	la oreja	*lah ohreh̲hah*
ear, nose and throat (ENT) specialist	el médico de oídos	*ehl mehdeekoh deh oheedohs*
earache	el dolor de oído	*ehl dohlohr deh oheedoh*
eardrops	las gotas para los oídos	*lahs gohtahs pahrah lohs oheedohs*
early	temprano	*tehmprahnoh*
earrings	los pendientes	*lohs pehndyehntehs*
earth	la tierra	*lah tyehrrah*
earthenware	la cerámica	*lah thehrahmeekah*
east	el este	*ehl ehsteh*
easy	fácil	*fahtheel*
eat	comer	*kohmehr*
eczema	el eczema	*ehl ehkthehmah*
eel	la anguila	*lah ahngeelah*
egg	el huevo	*ehl wehboh*
elastic band	la goma elástica	*lah gohmah ehlahsteekah*
electric	eléctrico	*ehlehktreekoh*
electricity	la corriente	*lah kohrryehnteh*
embassy	la embajada	*lah ehmbah̲hahdah*
emergency brake	el freno de emergencia	*ehl frehnoh deh ehmehr̲hehnthyah*

Word list

15

125

emergency exit	la salida de emergencia	*lah sahleedah deh ehmehrhehnthyah*
emergency number	el número de urgencias	*ehl noomehroh deh oorhehnthyahs*
emergency phone	el teléfono de emergencia	*ehl tehlehfohnoh deh ehmehrhehnthyah*
emergency triangle	el triángulo reflectante	*ehl treeahngooloh rehflehktahnteh*
emery board	la lima (para uñas)	*lah leemah (pahrah oonyahs)*
empty	vacío	*bahtheeoh*
engaged (phone)	comunicando	*kohmooneekahndoh*
engaged	ocupado	*ohkoopahdoh*
English	inglés	*eenglehs*
enjoy	disfrutar	*deesfrootahr*
entertainment guide	la guía de los espectáculos	*lah gheeah deh lohs ehspehktahkoolohs*
envelope	el sobre	*ehl sohbreh*
escort	el/la acompañante	*ehl/lah ahkohmpahnyahnteh*
evening	la tarde	*lah tahrdeh*
evening wear	el traje de etiqueta	*ehl trahheh deh ehteekehtah*
event	el acontecimiento	*ehl akohntehtheemyehntoh*
event (social)	la función	*lah foonthyohn*
everything	todo	*tohdoh*
everywhere	en todas partes	*ehn tohdahs pahrtehs*
examine	reconocer	*rehkohnohthehr*
excavation	las excavaciones	*lahs ehxkahbahthyohnehs*
excellent	excelente, estupendo	*ehxthehlehnteh, ehstoopehndoh*
exchange (verb)	cambiar	*kahmbyahr*
exchange office	la oficina de cambio	*lah ohfeetheenah deh kahmbyoh*
exchange rate	la cotización, el tipo de cambio	*lah kohteethahthyohn, ehl teepoh deh kahmbyoh*
excursion	la excursión organizada	*lah ehxkoorsyohn ohrgahneethahdah*
exhibition	la exposición	*lah ehxpohseethyohn*
exit	la salida	*lah sahleedah*
expenses	los gastos	*lohs gahstohs*
expensive	caro	*kahroh*
explain	explicar	*ehxpleekahr*
express train	el tren rápido	*ehl trehn rahpeedoh*
external	tópico, externo	*tohpeekoh, ehxtehrnoh*
eye	el ojo	*ehl ohhoh*
eye drops	las gotas para los ojos	*lahs gohtahs pahrah lohs ohhohs*
eye shadow	la sombra de ojos	*lah sohmbrah deh ohhohs*
eye specialist	el oculista	*ehl ohkooleestah*
eyeliner	el lápiz de ojos	*ehl lahpeeth deh ohhohs*

Word list

15

126

F

face	la cara	lah kahrah
factory	la fábrica	lah fahbreekah
fair	la feria	lah fehryah
fall	caer(se)	kahehr(seh)
family	la familia	lah fahmeelyah
famous	famoso	fahmohsoh
far away	lejos	leh<u>h</u>ohs
farm	la granja	lah grahn<u>h</u>ah
farmer	el campesino	ehl kahmpehseenoh
farmer's wife	la campesina	lah kahmpehseenah
fashion	la moda	lah mohdah
fast	rápido	rahpeedoh
father	el padre	ehl pahdreh
fault (blame)	la culpa	lah koolpah
fax (verb)	enviar un fax	ehnbyahr oon fahx
February	febrero	fehbrehroh
feel (verb)	sentir	sehnteer
feel like	apetecer	ahpehtehthehr
fence	la verja	lah behr<u>h</u>ah
ferry	el transbordador	ehl trahnsbohrdahdohr
fever	la fiebre	lah fyehbreh
fill (tooth)	empastar	ehmpahstahr
fill out	rellenar	rehlyehnahr
filling	el empaste	ehl ehmpahsteh
film (camera)	el rollo	ehl rohlyoh
film	la película	lah pehleekoolah
filter	el filtro	ehl feeltroh
find (verb)	encontrar	ehnkohntrahr
fine	la multa	lah mooltah
finger	el dedo	ehl dehdoh
fire	el fuego	ehl fwehgoh
fire (house etc.)	el incendio	ehl eenthehndyoh
fire brigade	los bomberos	lohs bohmbehrohs
fire escape	la escalera de incendios	lah ehskahlehrah deh eenthehndyohs
fire extinguisher	el extintor	ehl ehxteentohr
first	primero	preemehroh
first aid	los primeros auxilios	lohs preemehrohs ahooxeelyohs
first class	la primera clase	lah preemehrah klahseh
fish (verb)	pescar	pehskahr
fish	el pescado	ehl pehskahdoh
fishing rod	la caña de pescar	lah kanyah deh pehskahr
fitness centre	el gimnasio	ehl <u>h</u>eemnahsyoh
fitness training	la gimnasia	lah <u>h</u>eemnahsyah
fitting room	el probador	ehl prohbahdohr
fix puncture	arreglar el pinchazo	ahrrehglahr ehl peenchahthoh
flag	la bandera	lah bahndehrah
flamenco	el flamenco	ehl flahmehnkoh
flash cube	el cuboflash	ehl koobohflahsh
flash gun/bulb	el flash	ehl flahsh
flat	el piso	ehl peesoh

Word list

127

flea market	el mercadillo, el rastro	*ehl mehrkahdeelyoh, ehl rahstroh*
flight	el vuelo	*ehl bwehloh*
flight number	el número de vuelo	*ehl noomehroh deh bwehloh*
flood	la inundación	*lah eenoondathyohn*
floor	el piso	*ehl peesoh*
flour	la harina	*lah ahreenah*
flu	la gripe	*lah greepeh*
fly (insect)	la mosca	*lah mohskah*
fly (verb)	volar	*bohlahr*
fly-over	el viaducto	*ehl beeahdooktoh*
fog	la niebla	*lah nyehblah*
foggy (be)	haber niebla	*ahbehr nyehblah*
folkloristic	folclórico	*fohlklohreekoh*
follow	seguir	*sehgeer*
food	el alimento	*ehl ahleemehntoh*
food poisoning	la intoxicación alimenticia	*lah eentohxeekaht-hyohn ahleemehntee-thyah*
foodstuffs	los víveres	*lohs beebehrehs*
foot	el pie	*ehl pyeh*
for	antes, delante de	*ahntehs, dehlahnteh deh*
for hire	se alquila	*seh ahlkeelah*
forbidden	prohibido	*proheebeedoh*
forehead	la frente	*lah frehnteh*
foreign	extranjero	*ehxtrahn<u>h</u>ehroh*
forget	olvidar	*ohlbeedahr*
fork	el tenedor	*ehl tehnehdohr*
form	el formulario	*ehl fohrmoolahryoh*
fort	la fortificación	*lah fohrteefeekah-thyohn*
forward (send)	enviar	*ehnbyahr*
fountain	la fuente	*lah fwehnteh*
four-star petrol	súper	*soopehr*
frame	la montura	*lah mohntoorah*
free	libre	*leebreh*
free of charge	gratuito	*grahtweetoh*
free time	el tiempo libre	*ehl tyehmpoh leebreh*
freeze	helar	*ehlahr*
French	francés	*frahnthehs*
French bread	la barra de pan	*lah bahrrah deh pahn*
fresh	fresco	*frehskoh*
Friday	el viernes	*ehl byehrnehs*
fried	frito	*freetoh*
fried egg	el huevo al plato	*ehl wehboh ahl plahtoh*
friend	el amigo	*ehl ahmeegoh*
friendly	cordial, amable	*kohrdyahl, ahmahbleh*
frightened	miedoso	*myehdohsoh*
fringe	el flequillo	*ehl flehkeelyoh*
front (at the)	adelante	*ahdehlahnteh*
frozen goods	los productos congelados	*los prohdooktohs kohn<u>h</u>ehlahdohs*
fruit	la fruta	*lah frootah*
fruit juice	el zumo de frutas	*ehl thoomoh deh frootahs*

frying pan	la sartén	*lah sahrtehn*
full	lleno	*lyehnoh*
fun	la diversión	*lah deebehrsyohn*

G

gallery	la galería de arte	*lah gahlehreeah deh ahrteh*
game	el juego	*el hwehgoh*
garage (for repairs)	el taller mecánico	*ehl tahlyehr mehkahneekoh*
garbage bag	la bolsa de basura	*lah bohlsah deh bahsoorah*
garden	el jardín	*ehl hahrdeen*
gastroenteritis	la gastroenteritis	*lah gahstrohehnteh-reetees*
gauze	la gasa esterilizada	*lah gahsah ehstehreeleethahdah*
gear (bicycle)	el cambio	*ehl kahmbyoh*
gel	el gel	*ehl hehl*
German	alemán	*ahlehmahn*
get married	casarse	*kahsahrseh*
get off	bajarse	*bahhahrse*
gift	el regalo	*ehl rehgahloh*
gilt	dorado	*dohrahdoh*
ginger	el jengibre	*ehl hehnheebreh*
girl	la chica	*lah cheekah*
girlfriend	la amiga	*lah ahmeegah*
giro card	la tarjeta de la caja postal	*lah tahrhehtah deh lah kahhah pohstahl*
giro cheque	el cheque postal	*ehl chehkeh pohstahl*
glacier	el glaciar	*ehl glahthyahr*
glass (tumbler)	el vaso	*ehl bahsoh*
glass (wine -)	la copa	*lah kohpah*
glasses	las gafas	*lahs gahfahs*
glider	el vuelo sin motor	*ehl bwehloh seen mohtohr*
glove	el guante	*ehl gwahnteh*
glue	la cola	*lah kohlah*
gnat	el mosquito	*ehl mohskeetoh*
go (verb)	ir	*eer*
go back, come back	volver	*bohlbehr*
go backwards	ir para atrás	*eer pahrah ahtrahs*
go out	salir	*sahleer*
goat's cheese	el queso de cabra	*ehl kehsoh deh kahbrah*
gold	el oro	*ehl ohroh*
golf	el golf	*ehl gohlf*
golf course	el campo de golf	*ehl kahmpoh deh gohlf*
gone	perdido	*pehrdeedoh*
good afternoon	buenas tardes (after 2pm)	*bwehnahs tahrdehs*
good evening	buenas tardes	*bwehnahs tahrdehs*
good morning	buenos días (before 2pm)	*bwehnohs deeahs*
good night	buenas noches	*bwehnahs nohchehs*
goodbye	la despedida	*lah dehspehdeedah*
gram	el gramo	*ehl grahmoh*
grandchild	el nieto	*ehl nyehtoh*

Word list

15

129

grandfather	el abuelo	ehl ahbwehloh
grandmother	la abuela	lah ahbwehlah
grape juice	el zumo de uvas	ehl thoomoh deh oobahs
grapefruit	el pomelo	ehl pohmehloh
grapes	las uvas	lahs oobahs
grave	la tumba	lah toombah
grease	la grasa	lah grahsah
green	verde	behrdeh
green card	la tarjeta verde	lah tahrhehtah behrdeh
greet	saludar	sahloodahr
grey (hair)	canoso	kahnohsoh
grey	gris	grees
grill (verb)	asar a la parrilla	ahsahr ah lah pahreelyah
grilled	tostado	tohstahdoh
grocer's	la tienda de comestibles	lah tyehndah deh kohmehsteeblehs
ground	la tierra	lah tyehrrah
group	el grupo	ehl groopoh
guest house	la pensión	lah pehnsyohn
guide (book)	la guía	lah gueeah
guide (person)	el/la guía	ehl/lah gueeah
guided tour	la visita guiada	lah beeseetah gueeahdah
gynaecologist	el ginecólogo	ehl heenehkohlohgoh

H

hair	el pelo	ehl pehloh
hairbrush	el cepillo para el pelo	ehl thehpeelyoh parah ehl pehloh
hairdresser	la peluquería	lah pehlookehreeah
(ladies', men's)	(de señoras, caballeros)	(deh sehnyohrahs, kahbahlyehrohs)
hairpins	las horquillas	lahs ohrkeelyahs
hairspray	la laca para el pelo	lah lahkah pahrah ehl pehloh
half	medio, media, la mitad	mehdyoh, mehdyah, lah meetahdh
half full	lleno hasta la mitad	lyehnoh ahstah lah meetahdh
half kilo	el medio kilo	ehl mehdyoh keeloh
hammer	el martillo	ehl mahrteelyoh
hand	la mano	lah mahnoh
hand brake	el freno de mano	ehl frehnoh deh mahnoh
handbag	el bolso de mano	ehl bohlsoh deh mahnoh
handbag	el bolso	ehl bohlsoh
handkerchief	el pañuelo	ehl pahnywehloh
handmade	hecho a mano	ehchoh ah mahnoh
happy	contento	kohntehntoh
harbour	el puerto	ehl pwehrtoh
hard	duro	dooroh
haste	la prisa	lah preesah
hat	el sombrero	ehl sohmbrehroh

hay fever	la fiebre del heno	*lah fyehbreh dehl ehnoh*
hazelnut	la avellana	*lah ahbehlyahnah*
head	la cabeza	*lah kahbehthah*
headache	el dolor de cabeza	*ehl dohlohr deh kahbehthah*
health	la salud	*lah sahloodh*
health food shop	la tienda naturista	*lah tyehndah nahtooreestah*
hear	entender	*ehntehndehr*
hearing aid	el audífono	*ehl ahoodeefohnoh*
heart	el corazón	*ehl kohrahthohn*
heart patient	el enfermo cardíaco	*ehl ehnfehrmoh kahrdeeahkoh*
heat	calor	*kahlohr*
heater	la calefacción	*lah kahlehfahkthyohn*
heavy	pesado	*pehsahdoh*
heel	el talón	*ehl tahlohn*
heel (on shoe)	el tacón	*ehl tahkohn*
hello	hola	*ohlah*
helmet	el casco	*ehl kahskoh*
help (verb)	ayudar	*ahyoodahr*
help	la ayuda	*lah ahyoodah*
helping/portion	la ración	*lah rahthyohn*
herbal tea	la infusión	*lah eenfoosyohn*
here	aquí	*ahkee*
herring	el arenque	*ehl ahrehnkeh*
high	alto	*ahltoh*
high tide	la marea alta	*lah mahrehah ahltah*
highchair	la silla para niños	*lah seelyah pahrah neenyohs*
hiking	el excursionismo	*ehl ehxkoorsyohneesmoh*
hiking trip	la excursión a pie	*lah ehxkoorsyohn ah pyeh*
hip	la cadera	*lah kahdehrah*
hire	alquilar	*ahlkeelahr*
hitchhike	hacer autostop	*ahtehhr ahootohstohp*
hobby	el hobby	*ehl hohbee*
hold-up/robbery	el asalto	*ehl ahsahltoh*
holiday (public)	el día de fiesta	*ehl deeah deh fyehstah*
holiday house	el chalet	*ehl chahleh*
holiday park	la urbanización	*lah oorbahneethah-thyohn*
holidays	las vacaciones	*lahs bahkahthyohnehs*
home (at)	en casa	*ehn kahsah*
homesickness	la nostalgia	*lah nohstahlhyah*
honest	sincero	*seenthehroh*
honey	la miel	*lah myehl*
horizontal	horizontal	*oreethohntahl*
horrible	horrible	*ohrreebleh*
horse	el caballo	*ehl kahbahlyoh*
hospital	el hospital	*ehl ohspeetahl*
hospitality	la hospitalidad	*lah ohspeetahleedahdh*
hot	cálido/caluroso	*kahleedoh/ kahloorohsoh*
hot (spicy)	picante	*peekahnteh*

English	Spanish	Pronunciation
hotel	el hotel	*ehl ohtehl*
hot-water bottle	la bolsa de agua caliente	*lah bohlsah deh ahgwah kahlyehnteh*
hour	la hora	*lah ohrah*
house	la casa	*lah kahsah*
household items	los artículos del hogar	*lohs ahrteekoolohs dehl ohgahr*
houses of parliament	la cámara de diputados	*lah kahmahrah deh deepootahdohs*
housewife	el ama de casa	*ehl ahmah deh kahsah*
how far?	¿a qué distancia?	*ah keh deestahnthyah?*
how long?	¿cuánto tiempo?	*kwahntoh tyehmpoh?*
how much?	¿cuánto?	*kwahntoh?*
how?	¿cómo?	*kohmoh*
hunger	el hambre/el apetito	*ehl ahmbreh/ehl ahpehteetoh*
hurricane	el huracán	*ehl oorahkahn*
hurry	la prisa	*lah preesah*
husband	el marido	*ehl mahreedoh*
hut	el camarote	*ehl kahmahrohteh*
hyperventilation	la hiperventilación	*lah eepehr-behnteelahthyohn*

I

English	Spanish	Pronunciation
ice cream	el helado	*ehl ehlahdoh*
ice cubes	los cubitos de hielo	*lohs koobeetohs deh yehloh*
ice skating	el patinaje sobre hielo	*ehl pahteenahheh sohbreh yehloh*
idea	la idea	*lah eedehah*
identification card	el carnet de identidad	*ehl kahrneh deh eedehnteedahdh*
identify	identificar	*eedehnteefeekahr*
ignition key	la llave de contacto	*lah lyahbeh deh kohntahktoh*
ill	enfermo	*ehnfehrmoh*
illness	la enfermedad	*lah ehnfehrmehdahdh*
imagine	imaginarse	*eemahheenahrseh*
immediately	inmediatamente	*eenmehdyahtah-mehnteh*
import duty	los derechos de aduana	*lohs dehrehchohs deh ahdwahnah*
impossible	imposible	*eempohseebleh*
in	en	*ehn*
in the evening	por la tarde	*pohr lah tahrdeh*
in the morning	por la mañana	*pohr lah mahnyahnah*
included	incluido	*eenklooeedoh*
indicate	señalar	*sehnyahlahr*
indicator	el intermitente	*ehl eentehrmeetehnteh*
inexpensive	barato	*bahrahtoh*
infection (viral -, bacterial -)	la infección (vírica, bacteriana)	*lah eenfehkthyohn (beereekah, bahktehryahnah)*
inflammation	la inflamación	*lah eenflahmahthyohn*
information	la información	*lah eenfohrmahthyohn*
information office	la oficina de información	*lah ohfeetheenah deh eenfohrmahthyohn*

injection	la inyección	*lah eenyehkthyohn*
injured	herido	*erhreedoh*
inner ear	el oído	*ehl oheedoh*
inner tube	la cámara	*lah kahmahrah*
innocent	inocente	*eenohthehnteh*
insect	el insecto	*ehl eensehktoh*
insect bite	la picadura de insecto	*lah peekahdoorah deh eensehktoh*
insect repellant	el aceite para los mosquitos	*ehl ahthehyteh pahrah lohs mohskeetohs*
inside	adentro	*ahdehntroh*
insole	la plantilla	*lah plahnteelyah*
instructions	las instrucciones	*lahs eenstrookthyohnehs*
insurance	el seguro	*ehl sehgooroh*
intermission	la pausa	*lah pahoosah*
international	internacional	*eentehrnahthyohnahl*
interpreter	el intérprete	*ehl eentehrprehteh*
intersection/crossing	el cruce	*ehl krootheh*
introduce oneself	presentarse	*prehsehntahrseh*
invite (verb)	invitar	*eenbeetahr*
iodine	el yodo	*ehl yohdoh*
iron (metal)	el hierro	*ehl yehrroh*
iron (verb)	planchar	*plahnchahr*
iron	la plancha	*lah plahnchah*
ironing board	la tabla de planchar	*lah tahblah deh plahnchahr*
island	la isla	*lah eeslah*
it's a pleasure	de nada	*deh nahdah*
Italian	italiano	*eetahlyahnoh*
itch	la picazón	*lah peekahthohn*

J

jack	el gato	*ehl gahtoh*
jacket	la chaqueta	*lah chahkehtah*
jam	la mermelada	*lah mehrmehlahdah*
January	enero	*ehnehroh*
jaw	la mandíbula	*lah mahndeeboolah*
jellyfish	la medusa	*lah mehdoosah*
jeweller	la joyería	*lah hoyehreeah*
jewels	las alhajas	*lahs ahlahhahs*
jog (verb)	hacer footing	*ahtehr footeen*
joke	la broma	*lah brohmah*
journey	el viaje	*ehl byahheh*
juice	el zumo/el jugo	*ehl thoomoh/ehl hoogoh*
July	julio	*hoolyoh*
jump leads	el cable de arranque	*ehl kahbleh deh ahrrahnkeh*
jumper	el jersey	*ehl hehrsehee*
June	junio	*hoonyoh*

K

key	la llave	*lah lyahbeh*
kilo	el kilo	*ehl keeloh*
kilometre	kilómetro(s)	*keelohmehtroh(s)*
king	el rey	*ehl rehee*

kiss (verb)	besar	*behsahr*
kiss	el beso	*ehl behsoh*
kitchen	la cocina	*lah kohtheenah*
knee	la rodilla	*lah rohdeelyah*
knee socks	las medias cortas	*lahs mehdyahs kohrtahs*
knife	el cuchillo	*ehl koocheelyoh*
know	saber	*sahbehr*

L

lace	el encaje	*ehl ehnkahheh*
ladies'	el servicio para señoras	*ehl sehrbeethyoh pahrah sehnyohrahs*
lake	el lago	*ehl lahgoh*
lamp	la lámpara	*lah lahmpahrah*
land (verb)	aterrizar	*ahtehrreethahr*
lane	el carril	*ehl kahrreel*
language	el idioma	*ehl eedyohmah*
large	grande	*grahndeh*
last	pasado, último	*pahsahdoh, oolteemoh*
last night	anoche	*ahnohcheh*
late	tarde	*tahrdeh*
later	luego	*lwehgoh*
latest (at the)	a más tardar	*ah mahs tahrdahr*
laugh	reír	*reheer*
launderette	la lavandería (automática)	*lah lahbahndehreeah (ahootohmahteekah)*
law	el derecho	*ehl dehrehchoh*
laxative	el laxante	*ehl lahxahnteh*
leak	pinchado	*peenchahdoh*
leather	la piel, el cuero	*lah pyehl, ehl kwehroh*
leather goods	los artículos de piel	*lohs ahrteekoolohs deh pyehl*
leave (verb)	partir, salir	*pahrteer, sahleer*
leek	el puerro	*ehl pwehrroh*
left (on the)	a la izquierda	*ah lah eethkyehrdah*
left	izquierda	*eethkyehrdah*
left luggage	el depósito de equipajes	*ehl dehpohseetoh deh ehkeepahhehs*
leg	la pierna	*lah pyehrnah*
lemon	el limón	*ehl leemohn*
lemonade	la limonada	*lah leemohnahdah*
lend	prestar	*prehstahr*
lens	el objetivo	*ehl ohbhehteeboh*
lentils	las lentejas	*lahs lehntehhahs*
less	menos	*mehnohs*
lesson	la clase	*lah klahseh*
letter	la carta	*lah kahrtah*
lettuce	la lechuga	*lah lehchoogah*
level crossing	el paso a nivel	*ehl pahsoh ah neebehl*
library	la biblioteca	*lah beeblyohtehkah*
lie	mentir	*mehnteer*
lie down	estar tumbado	*ehstahr toombahdoh*
lift (hitchhike)	el viaje (en autostop)	*ehl byahheh (ehn ahootohstohp)*
lift (in building)	el ascensor	*ehl ahsthehnsohr*

lift (ski)	el telesquí, el telesilla	*ehl tehlehskee,ehl*
		tehlehseelyah
light (for cigarette)	el fuego	*ehl fwehgoh*
light (not dark)	claro	*klahroh*
light (not heavy)	ligero	*leehehroh*
lighter	el mechero	*ehl mehchehroh*
lighthouse	el faro	*ehl fahroh*
lightning	el rayo	*ehl rahyoh*
like	gustar	*goostahr*
line	la línea	*lah leenehah*
linen	el hilo	*ehl eeloh*
lipstick	la barra de labios	*lah bahrrah deh*
		lahbyohs
liqueur	la copa	*lah kohpah*
liquorice	el regaliz	*ehl rehgahleeth*
listen	escuchar	*ehskoochahr*
literature	la literatura	*lah leetehrahtoorah*
litre	el litro	*ehl leetroh*
little	poco	*pohkoh*
live (verb)	vivir	*beebeer*
live together	vivir con otra	*beebeer kohn ohtrah*
	persona	*pehrsohnah*
lobster	la langosta	*lah lahngohstah*
local	local	*lohkahl*
lock	la cerradura	*lah thehrrahdoorah*
long	largo	*lahrgoh*
look (verb)	mirar	*meerahr*
look for	buscar	*booskahr*
look up (person)	buscar	*booskahr*
lorry	el camión	*ehl kahmyohn*
lose	perder	*pehrdehr*
loss	la pérdida	*lah pehrdeedah*
lost (to get)	perderse, extraviarse	*pehrdehrseh,*
		ehxtrahbyahrseh
lost	extraviado, perdido	*ehxtrahbyahdoh,*
		pehrdeedoh
lost item	extravío	*ehxtrahbeeoh*
lost property office	los objetos perdidos	*lohs ohbhehtohs*
		pehrdeedohs
lotion	la loción	*lah lohthyohn*
loud	alto	*ahltoh*
love (be in - with)	estar enamorado de	*ehstahr*
		ehnahmohrahdoh deh
love (verb)	querer	*kehrehr*
love	el amor	*ehl ahmohr*
low	bajo	*bahhoh*
low tide	la marea baja	*lah mahrehah bahhah*
luck	la suerte	*lah swehrteh*
luggage	el equipaje	*ehl ehkeepahheh*
luggage locker	la consigna	*lah kohnseegnah*
	automática	*ahootohmahteekah*
lunch	el almuerzo, la	*ehl ahlmwehrthoh,*
	comida	*lah kohmeedah*
lungs	los pulmones	*lohs poolmohnehs*

M

macaroni	los macarrones	*lohs mahkahrrohnehs*
madam/Mrs	señora	*sehnyohrah*
magazine	la revista	*lah rehbeestah*
magnificent	magnífico	*mahgneefeekoh*
mail	el correo	*ehl kohrrehoh*
main post office	la oficina central de Correos	*ah ohfeetheenah thehntrahl deh kohrrehohs*
main road	la carretera principal	*lah kahrrehtehrah preentheepahl*
make an appointment	pedir hora	*pehdeer ohrah*
make love	acostarse/hacer el amor	*ahkohstahrseh/ahthehr ehl ahmohr*
makeshift	provisional(mente)	*prohbeesyohnahl (mehnteh)*
man	el hombre	*ehl ohmbreh*
manager	el encargado	*ehl ehnkahrgahdoh*
mandarin	la mandarina	*lah mahndahreenah*
manicure	la manicura	*lah mahneekoorah*
map	el mapa	*ehl mahpah*
marble	el mármol	*ehl mahrmohl*
March	marzo	*mahrthoh*
margarine	la margarina	*lah mahrgahreenah*
marina	el puerto deportivo	*ehl pwehrtoh dehpohrteeboh*
market	el mercado	*ehl mehrkahdoh*
marriage	el matrimonio	*ehl mahtreemohnyoh*
married	casado	*kahsahdoh*
mass	la misa	*lah meesah*
massage	el masaje	*ehl mahsahheh*
mat	mate	*mahteh*
matches	las cerillas	*lahs thehreelyahs*
May	mayo	*mahyoh*
maybe	quizá	*keethah*
mayonnaise	la mayonesa	*lah mahyohnehsah*
mayor	el alcalde	*ehl ahlkahldeh*
meal	la comida	*lah kohmeedah*
mean (verb)	significar	*seegneefeekahr*
meat	la carne	*lah kahrneh*
medical insurance	el seguro de enfermedad	*ehl sehgooroh deh ehnfehrmehdahdh*
medication	el medicamento	*ehl mehdeekahmehntoh*
medicine	el medicamento, la medicina	*ehl mehdeekahmehntoh, lah mehdeetheenah*
meet	conocer	*kohnohthehr*
melon	el melón	*ehl mehlohn*
membership	el ser socio	*ehl sehr sohthyoh*
menstruate	tener la regla	*tehnehr lah rehglah*
menstruation	la menstruación	*lah mehnstrooahthyohn*
menu	el menú, la carta	*ehl mehnoo, lah kahrtah*
menu of the day	el menú del día	*ehl mehnoo dehl deeah*
message	el recado/mensaje	*ehl rehkahdoh/ mehnsahheh*

metal	el metal	*ehl mehtahl*
meter (taxi)	el taxímetro	*ehl tahxeemehtroh*
metre	metro(s)	*mehtroh(s)*
migraine	la jaqueca	*lah hahkehkah*
mild (tobacco)	rubio	*roobyoh*
milk	la leche	*lah lehcheh*
millimetre(s)	milímetro(s)	*meeleemehtroh(s)*
milometer	el cuentakilómetros	*ehl kwehntah-keelohmehtrohs*
mince	la carne picada	*lah kahrneh peekahdah*
mineral water	el agua mineral	*ehl ahgwah meenehrahl*
minute	el minuto	*ehl meenootoh*
mirror	el espejo	*ehl ehspehoh*
miss (person)	echar de menos	*ehchahr deh mehnohs*
missing (be)	faltar	*fahltahr*
mistake	el error, la equivocación	*ehl ehrrohr, lah ehkeebohkahthyohn*
mistaken (be)	equivocarse	*ehkeebohkahrseh*
misunderstanding	el malentendido	*ehl mahlehntehndeedoh*
mixture	el jarabe, la poción	*ehl hahrahbeh, lah pohthyohn*
mocha	el moca	*ehl mohkah*
modern art	el arte moderno	*ehl ahrteh mohdehrnoh*
molar	la muela	*lah mwehlah*
moment	el momento	*ehl mohmehntoh*
Monday	el lunes	*ehl loonehs*
money	el dinero	*ehl deenehroh*
month	el mes	*ehl mehs*
moped	el ciclomotor	*ehl theeklohmohtohr*
morning-after pill	la píldora para el día después	*lah peeldohrah pahrah ehl deeah dehspwehs*
mosque	la mezquita	*lah methkeetah*
motel	el motel	*ehl mohtehl*
mother	la madre	*lah mahdreh*
motor cross	el motocrós	*ehl mohtohkrohs*
motorbike	la moto	*lah mohtoh*
motorboat	la lancha motora	*lah lahnchah mohtohrah*
motorway	la autovía, la autopista	*lah ahootohbeeah, lah ahootohpeestah*
mountain	la montaña	*lah mohntahnyah*
mountain hut	el refugio	*ehl rehfoohyoh*
mountaineering	el montañismo	*ehl mohntahnyeesmoh*
mountaineering shoes	las botas de alpinismo	*lahs bohtahs deh ahlpeeneesmoh*
mouse	el ratón	*ehl rahtohn*
mouth	la boca	*lah bohkah*
much/many	mucho	*moochoh*
multi-storey car park	el estacionamiento	*ehl ehstahthyohnah-myehntoh*
muscle	el músculo	*ehl mooskooloh*
muscle spasms	los calambres (en los músculos)	*lohs kahlahmbrehs (ehn lohs mooskoolohs)*
museum	el museo	*ehl moosehoh*
mushrooms	las setas	*lahs sehtahs*
music	la música	*lah mooseekah*

musical show	la comedia musical	*lah kohmehdyah mooseekahl*
mussels	los mejillones	*lohs meheelyohnehs*
mustard	la mostaza	*lah mohstahthah*

N

nail (on hand)	la uña	*lah oonyah*
nail	el clavo	*ehl klahboh*
nail polish	el esmalte (para uñas)	*ehl ehsmahlteh(pahrah oonyahs)*
nail polish remover	el quitaesmalte	*ehl keetahehsmahlteh*
nail scissors	las tijeras de uñas	*lahs teehehrahs pahrah oonyahs*
naked	desnudo	*dehsnoodoh*
nappy	el pañal	*ehl pahnyahl*
nationality	la nacionalidad	*lah nahthyohnahleedahdh*
nature	la naturaleza	*lah nahtoorahlehthah*
naturism	el naturismo	*ehl nahtooreesmoh*
nauseous	con náuseas	*kohn nahoosehahs*
near	junto a	*hoontoh ah*
nearby	cerca	*thehrkah*
necessary	necesario	*nehthehsahryoh*
neck	la nuca	*lah nookah*
necklace	la cadena	*lah kahdehnah*
needle	la aguja	*lah ahoohah*
negative	el negativo	*ehl nehgahteeboh*
neighbours	los vecinos	*lohs behtheenohs*
nephew	el sobrino	*ehl sohbreenoh*
Netherlands	los Países Bajos	*lohs paheesehs bahhohs*
never	jamás/nunca	*hahmahs/noonkah*
new	nuevo	*nwehboh*
news	las noticias	*lahs nohteethyahs*
news stand	el quiosco	*ehl kyohskoh*
newspaper	el periódico	*ehl pehryohdeekoh*
next	próximo, que viene	*prohxeemoh, keh byehnne*
next to	al lado de	*ahl lahdoh deh*
nice (friendly)	amable	*ahmahbleh*
nice (to look at)	bonito, mono	*bohneetoh, mohnoh*
nice	bien, agradable	*byehn, ahgrahdahbleh*
niece	la sobrina	*lah sohbreenah*
night (at)	por la noche	*pohr lah nohcheh*
night	la noche	*lah nohcheh*
night duty	la guardia nocturna	*lah gwahrdyah nohktoornah*
nightclub	el cabaré	*ehl kahbahreh*
nightlife	la vida nocturna	*lah beedah nohktoornah*
nipple	la tetina	*lah tehteenah*
no	no	*noh*
no overtaking	la prohibición de adelantar	*lah proheebeethyohn deh ahdehlahntahr*
noise	el ruido	*ehl rooeedoh*
nonstop	sin escalas	*seen ehskahlahs*
no-one	nadie	*nahdyeh*

normal	normal, corriente	*nohrmahl, kohrryehnteh*
north	el norte	*ehl nohrteh*
nose	la nariz	*lah nahreeth*
nose bleed	la hemorragia nasal	*lah ehmohrrah<u>h</u>yah nahsahl*
nose drops	las gotas para la nariz	*lahs gohtahs pahrah lah nahreeth*
notepaper	el papel de escribir	*ehl pahpehl deh ehskreebeer*
nothing	nada	*nahdah*
November	noviembre	*nohbyehmbreh*
nowhere	en ninguna parte	*ehn neengoonah pahrteh*
nudist beach	la playa nudista	*lah plahyah noodeestah*
number	el número	*ehl noomehroh*
number plate	la matrícula	*lah mahtreekoolah*
nurse	la enfermera	*lah ehnfehrmehrah*
nutmeg	la nuez moscada	*lah nwehth mohskahdah*
nuts	los frutos secos	*lohs frootohs sehkohs*

O

October	octubre	*ohktoobreh*
of course	claro	*klahroh*
off	podrido	*pohdreedoh*
offer	ofrecer	*ohfrehthehr*
office	la oficina	*lah ohfeetheenah*
off-licence	la bodega, la tienda de vinos y licores	*lah bohdehgah, lah tyehndah deh beenohs ee leekohrehs*
oil	el aceite	*ehl ahtheyteh*
oil level	el nivel del aceite	*ehl neebehl deh ahtheyteh*
ointment	la pomada, el ungüento	*lah pohmahdah, ehl oongwehntoh*
ointment for burns	la pomada contra las quemaduras	*lah pohmahdah kohntrah lahs kehmahdoorahs*
okay	vale, de acuerdo	*bahleh, deh ahkwehrdoh*
old	viejo	*byeh<u>h</u>oh*
old part of town	el casco antiguo	*ehl kahskoh ahnteegwoh*
olive oil	el aceite de oliva	*ehl ahtheyteh deh ohleebah*
olives	las aceitunas	*lahs ahtheytoonahs*
omelette	la tortilla	*lah tohrteelyah*
on	sobre	*sohbreh*
on board	a bordo	*ah bohrdoh*
oncoming car	el vehículo que viene	*ehl beheekooloh keh byehneh*
one hundred grams	los cien gramos	*lohs thyehn grahmohs*
one-way traffic	la dirección única	*lah deerehkthyohn ooneekah*
onion	la cebolla	*lah thehbohlyah*
open (adj.)	abierto	*ahbyehrtoh*
open (verb)	abrir	*ahbreer*

opera	la ópera	*lah ohpehrah*
operate	operar	*ohpehrahr*
operator (telephone)	la operadora	*lah ohpehrahdohrah*
operetta	la opereta, la zarzuela	*lah ohpehrehtah, lah thahrthwehlah*
opposite	al frente, enfrente de	*ahl frehnteh, ehnfrehnteh deh*
optician	la óptica	*lah ohpteekah*
orange	la naranja	*lah nahrahn<u>h</u>ah*
orange (adj.)	naranja	*nahrahn<u>h</u>a*
orange juice	el zumo de naranja	*ehl thoomoh deh nahrahn<u>h</u>ah*
order (in -,) tidy	en orden, ordenado	*ehn ohrdehn, ohrdehnahdo*
order (verb)	pedir	*pehdeer*
order	el pedido	*ehl pehdeedoh*
other	otro	*ohtroh*
other side	el otro lado	*ehl ohtroh lahdoh*
outside	afuera	*ahfwehrah*
overtake	adelantar	*ahdehlahntahr*
oysters	las ostras	*lahs ohstrahs*

P

packed lunch	el paquete con bocadillos	*ehl pahkehteh kohn bohkahdeelyohs*
page	la página	*lah pah<u>h</u>eenah*
pain	el dolor	*ehl dohlohr*
painkiller	el analgésico	*ehl ahnahl<u>h</u>ehseekoh*
paint (verb)	pintar	*peentahr*
paint	la pintura	*lah peentoorah*
painting (art)	el cuadro	*ehl kwahdroh*
painting (object)	la pintura	*lah peentoorah*
palace	el palacio	*ehl pahlahthyoh*
pancake	la crepe	*lah krehp*
pane	el cristal	*ehl kreestahl*
pants (briefs)	las bragas	*lahs brahgahs*
panty liner	el protegeslip	*ehl prohteh<u>h</u>ehsleep*
paper	el papel	*ehl pahpehl*
paraffin oil	el querosén	*ehl kehrohsehn*
parasol	el quitasol	*ehl keetahsohl*
parcel	el paquete	*ehl pahkehteh*
pardon	perdone	*pehrdohneh*
parents	los padres	*lohs pahdrehs*
park	el parque	*ehl pahrkeh*
park (verb)	aparcar	*ahpahrkahr*
parking space	el sitio para aparcar	*ehl seetyoh pahrah ahpahrkahr*
parsley	el perejil	*ehl pehreh<u>h</u>eel*
partition	la secreción	*lah sehkrehthyohn*
partner	la pareja	*lah pahreh<u>h</u>ah*
party	la fiesta	*lah fyehstah*
passable	practicable	*prahkteekahbleh*
passenger	el pasajero	*ehl pahsah<u>h</u>ehroh*
passport	el pasaporte	*ehl pahsahpohrteh*
passport photo	la foto de carnet	*lah fohtoh deh kahrneh*
patient	el paciente	*ehl pahthyehnteh*
pavement	la acera	*lah ahthehrah*

pay (verb)	pagar	*pahgahr*
pay the bill	pagar la cuenta	*pahgahr lah kwehntah*
peach	el melocotón	*ehl mehlohkohtohn*
peanuts	los cacahuetes	*lohs kahkahwehtehs*
pear	la pera	*lah pehrah*
peas	los guisantes	*lohs gueesahntehs*
pedal	el pedal	*ehl pehdahl*
pedestrian crossing	el paso de peatones	*ehl pahsoh deh pehahtohnehs*
pedicure	la pedicura	*lah pehdeekoorah*
pen	la pluma	*lah ploomah*
pencil (hard/soft)	el lápiz (duro/blando)	*ehl lahpeeth (dooroh /blahndoh)*
penis	el pene	*ehl pehneh*
pepper (capsicum)	el pimiento	*ehl peemyehntoh*
pepper (condiment)	la pimienta	*lah peemyehntah*
performance	la función de teatro /música	*lah foonthyohn deh tehahtroh/mooseekah*
perfume	el perfume	*ehl pehrfoomeh*
perm (verb)	hacer una permanente	*ahthehr oonah pehrmahnehnteh*
perm	la permanente	*lah pehrmahnehnteh*
permit	el permiso	*ehl pehrmeesoh*
person	la persona	*lah pehrsohnah*
personal	personal	*pehrsohnahl*
petrol	la gasolina	*lah gahsohleenah*
petrol station	la gasolinera	*lah gahsohleenehrah*
pets	los animales domésticos	*lohs ahneemahles dohmehsteekohs*
pharmacy	la farmacia	*lah fahrmahthyah*
phone (by)	por teléfono	*pohr tehlehfohnoh*
phone (tele-)	el teléfono	*ehl tehlehfohnoh*
phone (verb)	llamar por teléfono	*lyahmahr pohr tehlehfohnoh*
phone box	la cabina telefónica	*lah kahbeenah tehlehfohneekah*
phone directory	la guía de teléfonos	*lah gheeah deh tehlehfohnohs*
phone number	el número de teléfono	*ehl noomehroh deh tehlehfohnoh*
photo	la foto	*lah fohtoh*
photocopier	la fotocopiadora	*lah fohtohkohpyahdohrah*
photocopy (verb)	fotocopiar	*fohtohkohpyahr*
photocopy	la fotocopia	*lah fohtohkohpyah*
pick up (fetch person)	(ir a) buscar, pasar a buscar	*(eer ah) booskahr, pahsahr ah booskahr*
picnic	el picnic	*ehl peekneek*
piece of clothing	la prenda	*lah prehndah*
pier	el muelle	*ehl mwehlyeh*
pigeon	la paloma	*lah pahlohmah*
pill (contraceptive)	la píldora (anticonceptiva)	*lah peeldohrah (ahnteekohnthehp-teebah)*
pillow	la almohada	*lah ahlmohahdah*
pillowcase	la funda de almohada	*lah foondah deh ahlmohahdah*

pin	el alfiler	*ehl ahlfeelehr*
pineapple	la piña	*lah peenyah*
pipe	la pipa	*lah peepah*
pipe tobacco	el tabaco de pipa	*ehl tahbahkoh deh peepah*
pity	lástima	*lahsteemah*
place of entertainment	el sitio para salir	*ehl seetyoh pahrah sahleer*
place of interest	el punto de interés	*ehl poontoh deh eentehrehs*
plan/map	el plano	*ehl plahnoh*
plant	la planta	*lah plahntah*
plasters	las tiritas, los esparadrapos	*lahs teereetahs, lohs ehspahrah-drahpohs*
plastic	el plástico	*ehl plahsteekoh*
plastic bag	la bolsita	*lah bohlseetah*
plate	el plato	*ehl plahtoh*
platform	la vía, el andén	*lah beeah, ehl ahndehn*
play (theatre)	la obra de teatro	*lah ohbrah deh tehahtroh*
play (verb)	jugar	*hoogahr*
playground	el parque infantil	*ehl pahrkeh eenfahnteel*
playing cards	los naipes	*lohs naypehs*
pleasant	agradable	*ahgrahdahbleh*
please	por favor	*pohr fahbohr*
pleasure	el placer	*ehl plahthehr*
plum	la ciruela	*lah theerwehlah*
pocketknife	la navaja	*lah nahbahhah*
point (verb)	indicar	*eendeekahr*
poison	el veneno	*ehl behnehnoh*
police	la policía	*lah pohleetheeah*
police station	la comisaría	*la kohmeesahreeah*
policeman	el guardia	*ehl gwahrdyah*
pond	el estanque	*ehl ehstahnkeh*
pony	el poney	*ehl pohnehy*
pop concert	el concierto pop	*ehl kohnthyehrtoh pohp*
population	la población	*lah pohblahthyohn*
pork	la carne de cerdo	*lah kahrneh deh thehrdoh*
port wine	el oporto	*ehl ohpohrtoh*
porter	el portero	*ehl pohrtehroh*
post code	el código postal	*ehl cohdeegoh pohstahl*
post office	la oficina de Correos	*lah ohfeetheenah deh cohrrehohs*
postage	el franqueo	*ehl frahnkehoh*
postbox	el buzón	*ehl boothohn*
postcard	la (tarjeta) postal	*lah (tahrhehtah) pohstahl*
postman	el cartero	*ehl kahrtehroh*
potato	la patata	*lah pahtahtah*
poultry	las aves	*lahs ahbehs*
powdered milk	la leche en polvo	*lah lehcheh ehn pohlboh*

power point	la toma de corriente	*lah tohmah deh kohrryehnteh*
pram	el cochecito	*ehl kohchehtheetoh*
prawns	las gambas	*lahs gahmbahs*
precious	querido	*kehreedoh*
prefer	preferir	*prehfehreer*
preference	la preferencia	*lah prehfehrehnthyah*
pregnant	embarazada	*ehmbahrahthahdah*
present	presente	*prehsehnteh*
present (gift)	el regalo	*ehl rehgahloh*
press (verb)	apretar	*ahprehtahr*
pressure	la tensión	*lah tehnsyohn*
price	el precio	*ehl prehthyoh*
price list	la lista de precios	*lah leestah deh prehthyohs*
print (verb)	copiar	*kohpyahr*
print	la copia	*lah kohpyah*
probably	probablemente	*prohbahblehmehnteh*
problem	el problema	*ehl prohblehmah*
profession	la profesión	*lah prohfehsyohn*
programme	el programa	*ehl prohgrahmah*
pronounce	pronunciar	*prohnoonthyahr*
propane camping gas	el gas propano	*ehl gahs prohpahnoh*
pull	sacar	*sahkahr*
pull a muscle	distender un músculo	*deestehndehr oon mooskooloh*
pure	puro	*pooroh*
purple	violeta	*beeohlehta*
purse	el monedero	*ehl mohnehdehroh*
push	empujar	*ehmpoo<u>h</u>ahr*
puzzle	el rompecabezas	*ehl rohmpehkahbehthahs*
pyjamas	el pijama	*ehl pee<u>h</u>ahmah*

Q

quarter	la cuarta parte	*lah kwahrtah pahrteh*
quarter of an hour	el cuarto de hora	*ehl kwahrtoh deh ohrah*
queen	la reina	*lah reheenah*
question	la pregunta	*lah prehgoontah*
quick	rápido	*rahpeedoh*
quiet	tranquilo	*trahnkeeloh*

R

radio	la radio	*lah rahdyoh*
railways	los ferrocarriles	*lohs fehrrohkahrreelehs*
rain (verb)	llover	*lyohbehr*
rain	la lluvia	*lah lyoobyah*
raincoat	el impermeable	*ehl eempehrmehahbleh*
raisins	las uvas pasas	*lahs oobahs pahsahs*
rape	la violación	*lah beeohlahthyohn*
rapids	el rápido	*ehl rahpeedoh*
rash (skin)	la erupción cutánea	*lah ehroopthyohn kootahnehah*
raspberries	las frambuesas	*lahs frahmbwehsahs*
raw	crudo	*kroodoh*
raw ham	el jamón (serrano)	*ehl <u>h</u>ahmohn sehrrahnoh*

143

raw vegetables	las verduras crudas	lahs behrdoorahs kroodahs
razor blades	las hojas de afeitar	lahs _ohahs deh ahfeheetahr_
read (verb)	leer	lehehr
ready	listo	leestoh
really	en realidad	ehn rehahleedahdh
receipt	el recibo	ehl rehtheeboh
recipe	la receta	lah rehthehtah
reclining chair	la tumbona	lah toombohnah
recommend	recomendar	rehkohmehndahr
rectangle	el rectángulo	ehl rehktahngooloh
red	rojo	roh_h_oh
red wine	el vino tinto	ehl beenoh teentoh
refrigerator	el refrigerador	ehl rehfree_h_ehrahdohr
regards	recuerdos	rehkwehrdohs
region	la región	lah reh_h_yohn
registered	certificado	thehrteefeekahdoh
relatives	los parientes	lohs pahryehntehs
reliable	fiable/seguro	fyahbleh/sehgooroh
religion	la religión	lah rehlee_h_yohn
rent out	alquilar	ahlkeelahr
repair (verb)	arreglar	ahrrehglahr
repairs	el arreglo	ehl ahrrehgloh
repeat	repetir	rehpehteer
report	el atestado	ehl ahtehstahdoh
resent	tomar a mal	tohmahr ah mahl
responsible	responsable	rehspohnsahbleh
rest (verb)	descansar	dehskahnsahr
restaurant	el restaurante	ehl rehstahoorahnteh
retired	jubilado	_h_oobeeladoh
retirement	la jubilación	lah _h_oobeelahthyohn
return (ticket)	el billete de ida y vuelta	ehl beelyehteh deh eedah ee bwehltah
reverse (vehicle)	dar marcha atrás	dahr mahrchah ahtrahs
rheumatism	el reuma	ehl rehoomah
rice	el arroz	ehl ahrrohth
ridiculous	tontería(s)	tohntehreeah(s)
riding (horseback)	montar a caballo	mohntahr ah kahbahlyoh
riding school	el picadero	ehl peekahdehroh
right	derecha	dehrehchah
right (on the)	a la derecha	ah lah dehrehchah
right of way	la preferencia	lah prehfehrehnthyah
ripe	maduro	mahdooroh
risk	el riesgo	ehl ryehsgoh
river	el río	ehl reeoh
road	el camino	ehl kahmeenoh
roadway	la calzada	lah kahlthahdah
roasted	asado	ahsahdoh
rock	la roca	lah rohkah
rolling tobacco	el tabaco para liar	ehl tahbahkoh pahrah leeahr
roof rack	la baca	lah bahkah
room	la habitación	lah ahbeetahthyohn
room number	el número de la habitación	ehl noomehroh deh lah ahbeetahthyohn

room service	el servicio en la habitación	ehl sehrbeethyoh ehn lah ahbeetahthyohn
rope	la cuerda	lah kwehrdah
rosé	el vino rosado	ehl beenoh rohsahdoh
roundabout	la rotonda	lah rohtohndah
route	la ruta	lah rootah
rowing boat	el bote de remos	ehl bohteh deh rehmohs
rubber	la goma	lah gohmah
rubbish	tontería(s)	tohntehreeah(s)
rucksack	la mochila	lah mohcheelah
rude	descortés/ maleducado	dehskohrtehs/ mahlehdookahdoh
ruins	las ruinas	lahs rweenahs
run into	encontrar	ehnkohntrahr

S

sad	triste	treesteh
safari	el safari	ehl sahfahree
safe	la caja fuerte	lah kah<u>h</u>ah fwehrteh
safe/secure	seguro	sehgooroh
safety pin	el imperdible	ehl eempehrdeebleh
sail	la vela	lah behlah
sailing boat	el velero	ehl behlehroh
salad	la ensalada	lah ehnsahlahdah
salad oil	el aceite	ehl ahtehyteh
salami	el salami	ehl sahlahmee
sale	las rebajas, la liquidación	lahs rehbah<u>h</u>ahs, lah leekeedahthyohn
salt	la sal	lah sahl
same	mismo	meesmoh
same	lo mismo	loh meesmoh
sandwich	el bocadillo	ehl bohkahdeelyoh
sandy beach	la playa de arena	lah plahyah deh ahrehnah
sanitary towel	la compresa	lah kohmprehsah
sardines	las sardinas	lahs sahrdeenahs
satisfied	contento	kohntehntoh
Saturday	el sábado	ehl sahbahdoh
sauce	la salsa	lah sahlsah
saucepan	la cacerola	lah kahthehrohlah
sauna	la sauna	lah sahoonah
sausage	el embutido	ehl ehmbooteedoh
savoury	salado	sahlahdoh
say (verb)	decir	dehtheer
scarf	la bufanda (woollen)	lah boofahndah
scarf	el pañuelo	ehl pahnywehloh
scenic walk	la visita a la ciudad (a pie)	lah beeseetah ah lah thyoodahdh (ah pyeh)
school	la escuela	lah ehskwehlah
scissors	las tijeras	lahs tee<u>h</u>ehrahs
scooter	la vespa	lah behspah
scorpion	el escorpión	ehl ehskohrpyohn
scrambled eggs	los huevos revueltos	lohs wehbohs rehbwehltohs
screw	el tornillo	ehl tohrneelyoh

screwdriver	el destornillador	*ehl dehstohrneelyahdohr*
sculpture	la escultura	*lah ehskooltoorah*
sea	el mar	*ehl mahr*
seasick	mareado	*mahrehahdoh*
seat	el asiento	*ehl ahsyehntoh*
seat	el asiento, la butaca	*ehl ahsyehntoh, lah bootahkah*
second (adj.)	segundo	*sehgoondoh*
second	el segundo	*ehl sehgoondoh*
second-hand	de segunda mano	*deh sehgoondah mahnoh*
sedative	el calmante	*ehl kahlmahnteh*
see (person)	visitar	*beeseetahr*
see	mirar	*meerahr*
self-timer	el disparador automático	*ehl deespahrahdohr ahootohmahteekoh*
semi-skimmed	semidesnatado	*sehmeedehsnahtahdoh*
send	enviar	*ehnbyahr*
sentence	la frase	*lah frahseh*
September	septiembre	*sehptyehmbreh*
serious	grave	*grahbeh*
service	el servicio	*ehl sehrbeethyoh*
serviette	la servilleta	*lah sehrbeelyehtah*
set (verb)	marcar	*mahrkahr*
sewing thread	el hilo de coser	*ehl eeloh deh kohsehr*
shade	la sombra	*lah sohmbrah*
shallow	poco profundo	*pohkoh prohfoondoh*
shampoo	el champú	*ehl chahmpoo*
shark	el tiburón	*ehl teeboorohn*
shave (verb)	afeitar	*ahfeheetahr*
shaver	la afeitadora eléctrica	*lah ahfehytahdohrah ehlehkteekah*
shaving brush	la brocha de afeitar	*lah brohchah deh ahfeheetahr*
shaving cream	la crema de afeitar	*lah krehmah deh ahfeheetahr*
shaving soap	el jabón de afeitar	*ehl <u>h</u>ahbohn deh ahfeheetahr*
sheet	la sábana	*lah sahbahnah*
sherry	el jerez	*ehl <u>h</u>ehrehth*
shirt	la camisa	*lah kahmeesah*
shoe	el zapato	*ehl thahpahtoh*
shoe polish	la crema de zapatos	*lah krehmah deh thahpahtohs*
shoe shop	la zapatería	*lah thahpahtehreeah*
shoelaces	los cordones	*lohs kohrdohnehs*
shoemaker	el zapatero	*ehl thahpahtehroh*
shop (verb)	hacer la compra	*ahtehr lah kohmprah*
shop	la tienda	*lah tyehndah*
shop assistant	la vendedora	*lah behndehdohrah*
shop window	el escaparate	*ehl ehskahpahrahteh*
shopping centre	el centro comercial	*ehl thehntroh kohmehrthyahl*
short	corto	*kohrtoh*
short circuit	el cortocircuito	*ehl kohrtohtheer-kweetoh*

Word list

15

shoulder	el hombro	*ehl ohmbroh*
show	el espectáculo	*ehl ehspehktahkooloh*
shower	la ducha	*lah doochah*
shutter	el obturador	*ehl ohbtoorahdohr*
sieve	el tamiz	*ehl tahmeeth*
sign (verb)	firmar	*feermahr*
sign	el cartel	*ehl kahrtehl*
signature	la firma	*lah feermah*
signposted walk	la excursión	*lah ehxkooresyohn*
	señalizada	*sehnyahleethahdah*
silence	el silencio	*ehl seelehnthyoh*
silver	la plata	*lah plahtah*
silver-plated	plateado	*plahtehahdoh*
simple	sencillo	*sehntheelyoh*
single (unmarried)	soltero	*sohltehroh*
single	individual	*eendeebeedwahl*
single ticket	el billete de ida	*ehl beelyehteh deh*
		eedah
sir	señor	*sehnyohr*
sister	la hermana	*lah ehrmahnah*
sit	estar sentado	*ehstahr sehntahdoh*
size (shoes)	el número	*ehl noomehroh*
size	la talla	*lah tahlyah*
ski boots	las botas de esquí	*lahs bohtahs deh*
		ehskee
ski goggles	las gafas de esquí	*lahs gahfahs deh*
		ehskee
ski instructor	el profesor de esquí	*ehl prohfehsohr deh*
		ehskee
ski lessons/class	la clase de esquiar	*lah klahseh deh*
		ehskeeahr
ski lift	el telesquí	*ehl tehlehskee*
ski pants	los pantalones de	*lohs pahntahlohnehs*
	esquiar	*deh ehskeeahr*
ski pass	el bono (de remontes/	*ehl bohnoh (deh*
	esquí)	*rehmohntehs/ehskee)*
ski slope	la pista de esquí	*lah peestah deh*
	(alpino)	*ehskee (ahlpeenoh)*
ski stick	el bastón de esquí	*ehl bahstohn deh*
		ehskee
ski suit	el traje de esquiar	*ehl trahheh deh*
		ehskeeahr
ski wax	la cera para esquí	*lah thehrah pahrah*
		ehskee
ski/skiing	esquiar, el esquí	*ehskeeahr, ehl ehskee*
skin	la piel	*lah pyehl*
skirt	la falda	*lah fahldah*
skis	los esquís	*lohs ehskees*
sleep (verb)	dormir	*dohrmeer*
sleep well!	que descanse	*keh dehskahnseh*
sleeping car	el coche cama	*ehl kohcheh kahmah*
sleeping pills	los somníferos	*lohs sohmneefehrohs*
slide	la diapositiva	*lah deeahpohseeteebah*
slip (women's)	la combinación	*lah kohmbeenahthyohn*
slip road	la entrada	*lah ehntrahdah*
slow	despacio	*dehspahthyoh*
slow train	el tren ómnibus	*ehl trehn ohmneeboos*

Word list

15

147

small	pequeño	*pehkehnyoh*
small change	el cambio, el dinero suelto	*ehl kahmbyoh, ehl deenehroh swehltoh*
smell unpleasant (verb)	oler mal	*ohlehr mahl*
smoke	el humo	*ehl oomoh*
smoke (verb)	fumar	*foomahr*
smoked	ahumado	*ahoomahdoh*
smoking compartment	el departamento de fumadores	*ehl dehpahrtahmehntoh deh foomahdohrehs*
snake	la serpiente	*lah sehrpyehnteh*
snorkel	el esnórquel	*ehl ehsnohrkehl*
snow (verb)	nevar	*nehbahr*
snow	la nieve	*lah nyehbeh*
snow chains	la cadena antideslizante	*lah kahdehnah ahnteedehsleethahnte*
soap	el jabón	*ehl hahbohn*
soap box	la jabonera	*lah hahbohnehrah*
soap powder	el jabón en polvo	*ehl hahbohn ehn pohlboh*
soccer	el fútbol	*ehl footbohl*
soccer match	el partido de fútbol	*ehl pahrteedoh deh footbohl*
socket	el enchufe	*ehl ehnchoofeh*
socks	los calcetines	*lohs kahlthehteenehs*
soft drink	el refresco	*ehl rehfrehskoh*
sole (fish)	el lenguado	*ehl lehngwahdoh*
sole	la suela	*lah swehlah*
solicitor	el abogado	*ehl ahbohgahdoh*
someone	alguien	*ahlgyehn*
sometimes	a veces	*ah behthehs*
somewhere	en alguna parte	*ehn ahlgoonah pahrteh*
son	el hijo	*ehl eehoh*
soon	pronto	*prohntoh*
sorbet	el sorbete	*ehl sohrbehteh*
sore	la úlcera	*lah oolthehrah*
sore throat	el dolor de garganta	*ehl dohlohr deh gahrgahntah*
sorry	perdón	*pehrdohn*
sort/type	la clase	*lah klahseh*
soup	la sopa	*lah sohpah*
sour	agrio	*ahgreeoh*
sour cream	la nata ácida	*lah nahtah ahtheedah*
source	la fuente	*lah fwehnteh*
south	el sur	*ehl soor*
souvenir	el recuerdo de viaje	*ehl rehkwehrdoh deh byahheh*
spaghetti	los espaguetis	*lohs ehspahghehtees*
Spanish	español	*ehspahnyohl*
spanner (openended)	la llave (de boca)	*lah lyahbeh(deh bohkah)*
spanner	la llave de tuercas	*lah lyahbeh deh twehrkahs*
spare	la reserva	*lah rehsehrbah*
spare part	la pieza de recambio	*lah pyehthah deh rehkahmbyoh*
spare tyre	el neumático de reserva	*ehl nehoomahteekoh deh rehsehrbah*

spare wheel	la rueda de recambio	*lah rwehdah deh rehkahmbyoh*
speak	hablar	*ahblahr*
special	especial	*ehspehthyahl*
specialist	el especialista	*ehl ehspethyahleestah*
specialty	la especialidad	*lah ehspehthyahleedah*
speed limit	la velocidad máxima	*lah behlohtheedahdh mahxeemah*
spell (verb)	deletrear	*dehlehtrehahr*
spicy	picante	*peekahnteh*
splinter	la astilla	*lah ahsteelyah*
spoon	la cuchara	*lah koochahrah*
spoonful	la cucharada	*lah koochahrahdah*
sport (play)	hacer deporte	*ahthehr dehpohrteh*
sport	el deporte	*ehl dehpohrteh*
sports centre	la sala de deportes	*lah sahlah deh dehpohrtehs*
spot/place	el sitio	*ehl seetyoh*
sprain (verb)	torcerse	*tohrthehrseh*
spring	la primavera	*lah preemahbehrah*
square	el cuadrado	*ehl kwahdrahdoh*
square (town)	la plaza	*lah plahthah*
square metre(s)	metro(s) cuadrado(s)	*mehtroh(s) kwahdrahdoh(s)*
squash	el squash	*ehl skwahsh*
stadium	el estadio	*ehl ehstahdyoh*
stain	la mancha	*lah mahnchah*
stain remover	el quitamanchas	*ehl keetahmahnchahs*
stairs	las escaleras	*lahs ehskahlehrahs*
stalls (theatre)	la platea	*lah plahtehah*
stamp	el sello	*ehl sehlyoh*
start (car)	arrancar	*ahrrahnkahr*
station	la estación	*lah ehstahthyohn*
statue	la estatua	*lah ehstahtooah*
stay (lodge)	alojarse	*ahloh*h*ahrseh*
stay (verb)	quedarse	*kehdahrseh*
stay	la estancia	*lah ehstahnthyah*
steal (verb)	robar	*rohbahr*
steel, stainless	el acero, inoxidable	*ehl ahthehroh, eenohxeedahbleh*
stench	el mal olor	*ehl mahl ohlohr*
sting (verb)	picar	*peekahr*
stitch (med.)	el punto	*ehl poontoh*
stitch (verb)	suturar	*sootoorahr*
stock	el caldo	*ehl kahldoh*
stockings	las medias	*lahs mehdyahs*
stomach	el estómago, el vientre	*ehl ehstohmahgoh, ehl byehntreh*
stomach ache	el dolor de vientre/ estómago	*ehl dohlohr deh byehntreh/ ehstohmahgoh*
stomach cramps	los retortijones	*lohs rehtohrteeh*oh*nnehs*
stools	las heces	*lahs eh*th*ehs*
stop (verb)	parar	*pahrahr*
stop	la parada	*lah pahrahdah*
stopover	la escala	*lah ehskahlah*
storm	la tormenta	*lah tohrmehntah*

straight	liso	*leesoh*
straight ahead	todo recto	*tohdoh rehktoh*
straw	la pajita	*lah pah<u>h</u>eetah*
strawberries	las fresas	*lahs frehsahs*
street	la calle	*lah kahlyeh*
street side	el lado de la calle	*ehl lahdoh deh lah kahlyeh*
strike	la huelga	*lah wehlgah*
strong (tobacco)	negro	*nehgroh*
study (verb)	estudiar	*ehstoodyahr*
stuffing	el relleno	*ehl rehlyehnoh*
subscriber's number	el número de abonado	*ehl noomehroh deh ahbohnahdoh*
subtitled	subtitulada	*soobteetoolahdah*
succeed	salir bien	*sahleer byehn*
sugar	el azúcar	*ehl ahthookahr*
sugar lumps	los terrones de azúcar	*lohs tehrrohnehs deh ahthookahr*
suit	el traje	*ehl trah<u>h</u>eh*
suitcase	la maleta	*lah mahlehtah*
summer	el verano	*ehl behrahnoh*
summertime	la hora de verano	*lah ohrah deh behrahnoh*
sun	el sol	*ehl sohl*
sun hat	el sombrero de playa	*ehl sohmbrehroh deh plahyah*
sunbathe	tomar el sol	*tohmahr ehl sohl*
Sunday	el domingo	*ehl dohmeengoh*
sunglasses	las gafas de sol	*lahs gahfahs deh sohl*
sunrise	la salida del sol	*lah sahleedah dehl sohl*
sunset	la puesta del sol	*lah pwehstah dehl sohl*
sunstroke	la insolación	*lah eensohlahthyohn*
suntan lotion	la crema solar	*lah krehmah sohlahr*
suntan oil	el aceite bronceador	*ehl ahthehyteh brohnthehahdohr*
supermarket	el supermercado	*ehl soopehrmehrkahdoh*
surcharge	el suplemento	*ehl sooplehmehntoh*
surf	el surf	*ehl soorf*
surf board	la tabla de surf	*lah tahblah deh soorf*
surgery	la consulta	*lah kohnsooltah*
surname	el apellido	*ehl ahpehlyeedoh*
surprise	la sorpresa	*lah sohrprehsah*
swallow (verb)	tragar	*trahgahr*
swamp	el terreno pantanoso	*ehl tehrrehnoh pahntahnohsoh*
sweat	el sudor	*ehl soodohr*
sweet	el caramelo	*ehl kahrahmehloh*
sweet	dulce	*dooltheh*
sweetcorn	el maíz	*ehl maheeth*
sweetener	la sacarina	*lah sahkahreenah*
sweets	las golosinas	*lahs gohlohseenahs*
swim (verb)	nadar	*nahdahr*
swimming pool	la piscina	*lah peestheenah*
swimming trunks	el bañador	*ehl bahnyahdohr*
swindle	la estafa	*lah ehstahfah*
switch	el interruptor	*ehl eentehrrooptohr*

Word list

15

| synagogue | la sinagoga | *lah seenahgohgah* |

T

table	la mesa	*lah mehsah*
table tennis	el pingpong	*ehl peenpohn*
tablet	la tableta	*lah tahblehtah*
take (photograph)	sacar	*sahkahr*
take (time)	durar, tardar	*doorahr, tahrdahr*
take (verb)	emplear, usar, tomar	*ehmplehahr, oosahr, tohmahr*
take pictures	fotografiar, sacar fotos	*fohtohgrahfyahr, sahkahr fohtohs*
taken	ocupado	*ohkoopahdoh*
talcum powder	el talco	*ehl tahlkoh*
talk (verb)	hablar	*ahblahr*
tampons	los tampones	*lohs tahmpohnehs*
tap	el grifo	*ehl greefoh*
tap water	el agua del grifo	*ehl ahgwah dehl greefoh*
tart	la tarta	*lah tahrtah*
taste (verb)	probar	*prohbahr*
tax free shop	la tienda libre de impuestos	*lah tyehndah leebreh deh eempwehstohs*
taxi	el taxi	*ehl tahxee*
taxi stand	la parada de taxis	*lah pahrahdah deh tahxees*
tea	el té	*ehl teh*
teapot	la tetera	*lah tehtehrah*
teaspoon	la cuchara de té	*lah koochahrah deh teh*
telegram	el telegrama	*ehl tehlehgrahmah*
telephoto lens	el teleobjetivo	*ehl tehlehohbhehteeboh*
television	la televisión	*lah tehlehbeesyohn*
telex	el télex	*ehl tehlehx*
temperature	la temperatura	*lah tehmpehrahtoorah*
temporary filling	el empaste provisional	*ehl ehmpahsteh prohbeesyohnahl*
tender	tierno	*tyehrnoh*
tennis	el tenis	*ehl tehnees*
tennis ball	la pelota de tenis	*lah pehlohtah deh tehnees*
tennis court	la pista de tenis	*lah peestah deh tehnees*
tennis racket	la raqueta de tenis	*lah rahkehtah deh tehnees*
tennis shoes	los zapatos de tenis	*lohs thahpahtohs deh tehnees*
tenpin bowling	los bolos	*lohs bohlohs*
tent	la tienda	*lah tyehndah*
tent peg	la estaca	*lah ehstahkah*
terrace	la terraza	*lah tehrrahthah*
terrible	terrible	*tehrreebleh*
thank (verb)	agradecer	*ahgrahdehthehr*
thank you	gracias	*grahthyahs*
thaw	deshelar	*dehsehlahr*
the day after tomorrow	pasado mañana	*pahsahdoh mahnyahnah*

Word list

15

theatre	el teatro	*ehl tehahtroh*
theft	el robo	*ehl rohboh*
there	allí	*ahlyee*
thermal bath	el baño termal	*ehl bahnyoh tehrmahl*
thermometer	el termómetro	*ehl tehrmohmehtroh*
thick	grueso/gordo	*grwehsoh/gohrdoh*
thief	el ladrón	*ehl lahdrohn*
thigh	el muslo	*ehl moosloh*
thin	fino, flaco	*feenoh, flahkoh*
things	las cosas	*lahs kohsahs*
think	pensar	*pehnsahr*
third	la tercera parte	*lah tehrthehrah pahrteh*
thirsty, to be	la sed	*lah sehd*
this afternoon	esta tarde	*ehstah tahrdeh*
this evening	esta noche	*ehstah nohcheh*
this morning	esta mañana	*ehstah mahnyahnah*
thread	el hilo	*ehl eeloh*
throat	la garganta	*lah gahrgahntah*
throat lozenges	las pastillas para la garganta	*lahs pahsteelyahs pahrah lah gahrgahntah*
throw up	vomitar	*bohmeetahr*
thunderstorm	la tormenta eléctrica	*lah tohrmehntah ehlehktreekah*
Thursday	el jueves	*ehl <u>h</u>wehbehs*
ticket (admission)	la entrada	*lah ehntrahdah*
ticket (travel)	el billete	*ehl beelyehteh*
tickets	los billetes	*lohs beelyehtehs*
tidy (verb)	recoger	*rehko<u>h</u>ehr*
tie	la corbata	*lah kohrbahtah*
tights	el leotardo, el panty	*ehl lehohtahrdoh, ehl pahntee*
time (occasion)	la vez	*lah behth*
time	el tiempo	*ehl tyehmpoh*
timetable	el horario	*ehl ohrahryoh*
tin	la lata	*lah lahtah*
tip (money)	la propina	*lah prohpeenah*
tissues	los pañuelitos de papel	*lohs pahnywehleetohs de pahpehl*
toast	el pan tostado, las tostadas	*ehl pahn tohstahdoh, lahs tohstahdahs*
tobacco	el tabaco	*ehl tahbahkoh*
toboggan	el trineo	*ehl treenehoh*
today	hoy	*oy*
toe	el dedo del pie	*ehl dehdoh dehl pyeh*
together	juntos	*<u>h</u>oontohs*
toilet	el water/los servicios/ el lavabo	*ehl bahtehr/lohs sehrbeethyohs, ehl lahbahboh*
toilet paper	el papel higiénico	*ehl pahpehl ee<u>h</u>yehneekoh*
toiletries	los artículos de tocador	*lohs ahrteekoolohs deh tohkahdohr*
tomato	el tomate	*ehl tohmahteh*
tomato purée	el tomate triturado	*ehl tohmahteh treetoorahdoh*
tomato sauce	el ketchup	*ehl kehchoop*
tomorrow	mañana	*mahnyahnah*

tongue	la lengua	*lah lehngwah*
tonic water	el agua tónica	*ehl agwah tohneekah*
tonight	esta noche	*ehstah nohcheh*
too much	demasiado	*dehmahsyahdoh*
tools	las herramientas	*lahs ehrrahmyehntahs*
tooth	el diente	*ehl dyehnteh*
toothache	el dolor de muelas	*ehl dohlohr deh mwehlahs*
toothbrush	el cepillo de dientes	*ehl thehpeelyoh deh dyehntehs*
toothpaste	el dentífrico	*ehl dehnteefreekoh*
toothpick	el palillo	*ehl pahleelyoh*
top up	rellenar	*rehlyehnahr*
total	el total	*ehl tohtahl*
tough	duro	*dooroh*
tour	la excursión, el paseo	*lah ehxkoorsyohn, ehl pahsehoh*
tour guide	el guía	*ehl gheeah*
tourist card	la tarjeta de turista	*lah tahr<u>h</u>ehtah deh tooreestah*
tourist class	la clase turista	*lah klahseh tooreestah*
Tourist Information office	la oficina de (información y) turismo	*lah ohfeetheenah deh (eenfohrmahthyohn ee) tooreesmoh*
tourist menu	el menú turístico	*ehl mehnoo tooreesteekoh*
tow	remolcar	*rehmohlkahr*
tow cable	el cable de remolque	*ehl kahbleh deh rehmohlkeh*
towel	la toalla	*lah tohahlyah*
tower	la torre	*lah tohrreh*
town hall	el ayuntamiento	*ehl ahyoontahmyehntoh*
town/city	la ciudad	*lah thyoodahdh*
toys	los juguetes	*lohs <u>h</u>oogehtehs*
traffic	el tráfico	*ehl trahfeekoh*
traffic light	el semáforo	*ehl sehmahfohroh*
trailer tent	el remolque tienda	*ehl rehmohlkeh tyehndah*
train	el tren	*ehl trehn*
train ticket	el billete de tren	*ehl beelyehteh deh trehn*
train timetable	la guía de trenes	*lah gueeah deh trehnehs*
translate	traducir	*trahdootheer*
travel (verb)	viajar	*byah<u>h</u>ahr*
travel agent	la agencia de viajes	*lah ah<u>h</u>ehnthyah deh byah<u>h</u>ehs*
travel guide	la guía	*lah gheeah*
traveller	el pasajero	*ehl pahsah<u>h</u>ehroh*
traveller's cheque	el cheque de viajero	*ehl chehkeh deh byah<u>h</u>ehroh*
treacle/syrup	la melaza	*lah mehlahthah*
treatment	el tratamiento	*ehl trahtahmyehntoh*
triangle	el triángulo	*ehl treeahngooloh*
trim	cortar las puntas	*kohrtahr lahs poontahs*

Word list

15

trip	el paseo, la excursión	_ehl pahsehoh, lah_
		ehxkoorsyohn
trouble	la molestia	_lah mohlehstyah_
trousers (long, short)	los pantalones	_lohs pahntahlohnehs_
	(cortos, largos)	_(kohrtohs, lahrgohs)_
trout	la trucha	_lah troochah_
trunk call	interurbano	_eentehroorbahnoh_
trunk code	el prefijo	_ehl prehfeehoh_
trustworthy	digno de confianza	_deegnoh deh_
		kohnfyahnthah
try on (clothes)	probarse	_prohbahrse_
T-shirt	la camiseta	_lah kahmeesehtah_
tube	el tubo	_ehl tooboh_
Tuesday	el martes	_ehl mahrtehs_
tumble drier	la secadora	_lah sehkahdohrah_
tuna	el atún	_ehl ahtoon_
tunnel	el túnel	_ehl toonehl_
turn	la vez	_lah behth_
TV	la televisión	_lah tehlehbeesyohn_
tv and radio guide	la guía de radio y	_lah gheeah deh rahdyoh_
	televisión	_ee tehlehbeesyohn_
tweezers	los alicates	_lohs ahleekahtehs_
tyre (bicycle)	la cubierta	_lah koobyehrtah_
tyre lever	el desmontador de	_ehl dehsmohntahdohr_
	neumáticos	_deh nehoomahteekohs_
tyre pressure	la presión de los	_lah prehsyohn deh lohs_
	neumáticos	_nehoomahteekohs_

U

ugly	feo	_fehoh_
umbrella	el paraguas	_ehl pahrahgwahs_
under	abajo, debajo de	_ahbahhoh, dehbahhoh_
		deh
underground railway	el metro	_ehl mehtroh_
underground railway	la red de metro	_lah rehdh deh mehtroh_
system		
underground station	la estación de metro	_lah ehstahthyohn deh_
		mehtroh
underpants	los calzoncillos	_lohs_
		kahlthohntheelyohs
understand	entender	_ehntehndehr_
underwear	la ropa interior	_lah rohpah eentehryohr_
undress (verb)	desvestirse	_dehsbehsteerseh_
unemployed	en paro	_ehn pahroh_
uneven	desigual	_dehseegwahl_
university	la universidad	_lah ooneebehrseedah_
unleaded	sin plomo	_seen plohmoh_
urgent	urgente	_oorhehnteh_
urine	la orina	_lah ohreenah_
usually	por lo general	_pohr loh hehnehrahl_

V

vacate	desalojar	_dehsahlohhahr_
vaccinate	vacunarse	_bahkoonahrse_
vagina	la vagina	_lah bahheenah_
vaginal infection	la infección vaginal	_lah eenfehkthyohn_
		bahheenal

valid	válido	*bahleedoh*
valley	el valle	*ehl bahlyeh*
valuable	costoso	*kohstohsoh*
van	la furgoneta	*lah foorgohnehtah*
vanilla	la vainilla	*lah baheeneelyah*
vase	el florero	*ehl flohrehroh*
vaseline	la vaselina	*lah bahsehleenah*
veal	la carne de ternera	*lah kahrneh deh tehrnehrah*
vegetable soup	la sopa de verduras	*lah sohpah deh behrdoorahs*
vegetables	la verdura	*lah behrdoorah*
vegetarian	vegetariano	*behhehtahryahnoh*
vein	la vena	*lah vehnah*
vending machine	la máquina automática	*lah mahkeenah ahootohmahteekah*
venereal disease	la enfermedad venérea	*lah ehnfehrmehdahdh behnehrehah*
via	pasando por	*pahsahndoh pohr*
video recorder	el video	*ehl beedehoh*
video tape	la cinta de vídeo	*lah theentah deh beedehoh*
view	la vista	*lah beestah*
village	el pueblo	*ehl pwehbloh*
visa	el visado	*ehl beesahdoh*
visit (verb)	visitar	*beeseetahr*
visit	la visita	*lah beeseetah*
vitamin tablets	las tabletas de vitaminas	*lahs tahblehtahs deh beetahmeenahs*
vitamins	la vitamina	*lah beetahmeenah*
volcano	el volcán	*ehl bohlkahn*
volleyball (play)	jugar al vóleibol	*hoogahr ahl bohleheebohl*
vomit (verb)	vomitar	*bohmeetahr*

W

wait (verb)	esperar	*ehspehrahr*
waiter	el camarero	*ehl kahmahrehroh*
waiting room	la sala de espera	*lah sahlah deh ehspehrah*
waitress	la camarera	*lah kahmahrehrah*
wake up (verb)	despertar	*dehspehrtahr*
walk	el paseo	*ehl pahsehoh*
walk (take a)	salir a caminar	*sahleer ah kahmeenahr*
walk (verb)	ir (andando)	*eer(ahndahndoh)*
wallet	la cartera	*lah kahrtehrah*
wardrobe	el guardarropa	*ehl gwahrdahrrohpah*
warm	caliente	*kahlyehnteh*
warn	avisar, llamar	*ahbeesahr,lyahmahr*
warning	el aviso	*ehl ahbeesoh*
wash (verb)	lavar	*lahbahr*
washing (dirty)	la ropa sucia	*lah rohpah soothyah*
washing line	la cuerda de colgar la ropa	*lah kwehrdah deh kohlgahr lah rohpah*
washing machine	la lavadora	*lah lahbahdohrah*
washing-powder	el detergente	*ehl dehtehrhehnteh*
wasp	la avispa	*lah ahbeespah*

Word list

15

155

watch	el reloj	*ehl rehloh*
water	el agua	*ehl ahgwah*
water ski	el esquí acuático	*ehl ehskee ahkwahteekoh*
waterproof	impermeable	*eempehrmehahbleh*
wave-pool	la piscina con oleaje	*lah peestheenah kohn ohlehahheh*
way (means)	el remedio	*ehl rehmehdyoh*
way (on the)	en el camino	*ehn ehl kahmeenoh*
way	el lado	*ehl lahdoh*
we	nosotros	*nohsohtrohs*
weak	débil	*dehbeel*
weather	el tiempo	*ehl tyehmpoh*
weather forecast	el pronóstico del tiempo	*ehl prohnohsteekoh dehl tyehmpoh*
wedding	la boda	*lah bohdah*
Wednesday	el miércoles	*ehl myehrkohlehs*
week	la semana	*lah sehmahnah*
weekend	el fin de semana	*ehl feen deh sehmahnah*
weekend duty	la guardia de fin de semana	*lah gwahrdyah deh feen deh sehmahnah*
weekly ticket	el abono semanal	*ehl ahbohnoh sehmahnahl*
welcome	bienvenido	*byehnbehneedoh*
well	bien, bueno	*byehn, bwehnoh*
west	el oeste	*ehl ohehsteh*
wet	mojado	*mohahdoh*
wet (weather)	lluvioso	*lyoobyohsoh*
wetsuit	el traje de surf	*ehl trahheh deh soorf*
what?	¿qué?	*keh?*
wheel	la rueda	*lah rwehdah*
wheelchair	la silla de ruedas	*lah seelyah deh rwehdahs*
when?	¿cuándo?	*kwahndoh?*
where?	¿dónde?	*dohndeh?*
which?	¿cuál?	*kwahl?*
whipped cream	el chantilly	*ehl chahnteelyee*
whipping cream	la nata para batir	*lah nahtah pahrah bahteer*
white	blanco	*blahnkoh*
who?	¿quién?	*kyehn?*
wholemeal	integral	*eentehgrahl*
wholemeal bread	el pan integral	*ehl pahn eentehgrahl*
why?	¿por qué?	*pohr keh?*
wide-angle lens	el objetivo gran angular	*ehl obhehteeboh grahn ahngoolahr*
widow	la viuda	*lah byoodah*
widower	el viudo	*ehl byoodoh*
wife	la mujer	*lah moohehr*
wind	el viento	*ehl byehntoh*
windbreak	la protección contra el viento	*lah prohtehkthyohn kohntrah ehl byehntoh*
windmill	el molino	*ehl mohleenoh*
window	la ventanilla, la ventana	*lah behntahneelyah, lah behntahnah*

windscreen wiper	el limpiaparabrisas	*ehl leempyahpahrah-breesahs*
wine	el vino	*ehl beenoh*
wine list	la carta de vinos	*lah kahrtah deh beenohs*
winter	el invierno	*ehl eenbyehrnoh*
witness	el testigo	*ehl tehsteegoh*
woman	la mujer	*lah moohehr*
wood	la madera	*lah mahdehrah*
wool	la lana	*lah lahnah*
word	la palabra	*lah pahlahbrah*
work	el trabajo	*ehl trahbahhoh*
working day	el día laborable	*ehl deeah lahbohrahbleh*
worn/used	gastado	*gahstahdoh*
worried	inquieto	*eenkyehtoh*
wound	la herida	*lah ehreedah*
wrap (verb)	envolver	*ehnbohlbehr*
wrist	la muñeca	*lah moonyehkah*
write	escribir	*ehskreebeer*
write down	apuntar	*ahpoontahr*
writing pad	el bloc (cuadriculado, a rayas)	*ehl blohk(kwahdreekoolahdoh, ah rahyahs)*
writing paper	el papel de escribir	*ehl pahpehl deh ehskreebeer*
written	por carta	*pohr kahrtah*
wrong	mal, equivocado	*mahl, ehkeebohkahdoh*

Y

yacht	el yate	*ehl yahteh*
year	el año	*ehl anyoh*
yellow	amarillo	*ahmahreelyoh*
yes	sí	*see*
yes, please	con (mucho) gusto	*kohn (moochoh) goostoh*
yesterday	ayer	*ahyehr*
yoghurt	el yogur	*ehl yohgoor*
you (formal)	usted	*oostehdh*
you too	igualmente	*eegwahlmehnteh*
youth hostel	el albergue juvenil	*ehl ahlbehrgeh hoobehneel*

Z

| zip | la cremallera | *lah krehmahlyehrah* |
| zoo | el parque zoológico | *ehl pahrkeh thohohlohheekoh* |

Word list

15

Basic grammar

1 The article

Spanish nouns and adjectives are divided into 2 categories: masculine and feminine. The definite article (the) is **el** or **la**. Most masculine words end in **o** and most feminine words end in **a**.

el is used before masculine nouns, as in **el tren** (the train)
la is used before feminine nouns, as in **la playa** (the beach)
el is also used before feminine nouns beginning with a vowel, as in **el agua** (water).

Other examples are:

el techo	the roof	**la casa**	the house
el hambre	hunger	**el alma**	the soul

The plural of **el** is **los**; the plural of **la** is **las**.

In the case of the indefinite article (**a, an**):

un is used before masculine nouns, as in **un libro** (a book).

una is used before feminine nouns, as in **una mesa** (a table).

The plural is constructed by adding s, as in **unos camiones** (some lorries), **unas tazas** (some cups).

Other examples are:

un padre	a father	**una madre**	a mother
un hombre	a man	**una mujer**	a woman
unos hombres	men	**unas mujeres**	women

2 The plural

The plural of Spanish nouns and adjectives ends in **s**. Examples are:

singular	plural
el avión (the plane)	**los aviones**
la manzana (the apple)	**las manzanas**

3 Personal pronouns

I	**yo**
You	**tú/Usted**
He/she/it	**él/ella**
We	**nosotros/nosotras**
You	**vosotros/vosotras/Ustedes**
They	**ellos/ellas**

When speaking to a person one does not know well, **Usted** is used with the third person of the verb:

e.g. **Usted sabe/Ustedes saben**   you know

4 Possessive pronouns

	masculine/feminine	plural
my	**mi**	**mis**
your	**tu**	**tus**
his/her/its	**su**	**sus**
our	**nuestro/nuestra**	**nuestros/nuestras**
your	**vuestro/vuestra**	**vuestros/vuestras**
their	**su**	**sus**

They agree with the object they modify, e.g. our car = **nuestro coche**.

5 Verbs

Note: pronouns are only used with verbs when absolutely necessary.

hablar	to speak
hablo	I speak
hablas	you speak
habla	he/she/you speak
hablamos	we speak
habláis	you speak
hablan	they/you speak

Here are some useful verbs:

ser	**estar** (to be)
soy	**estoy**
eres	**estás**
es	**está**
somos	**estamos**
sois	**estáis**
son	**están**

Note: **estar** is used with places and also means a temporary state, e.g. **el hotel está en la plaza**, (the hotel is in the square), **la niña está cansada** (the little girl is tired).

tener (to have)	**hacer** (to do/make)
tengo	**hago**
tienes	**haces**
tiene	**hace**
tenemos	**hacemos**
tenéis	**hacéis**
tienen	**hacen**

ir (to go)	**ver** (to see)
voy	**veo**
vas	**ves**
va	**ve**
vamos	**vemos**
vais	**veis**
van	**ven**

Negatives are formed by putting no before the verb:
e.g. **no entiendo**, I do not understand; **no oigo**, I cannot hear.

6 Basic prepositions

a = to, e.g. **voy a Madrid, voy al mercado**.
en= in or at, e.g. **estoy en la tienda, estoy en casa**.